"*How Much Is Enough?* is a nonviolent assault on consumerism, written, as it is, more in hope than in anger. It is a profound and moving book, full of biblical insights informing both our personal behavior and public policies, that in short order could change the world to a more just and peaceful place."

—Rev. William Sloane Coffin

"We have waited too long for this book—since the election of Ronald Reagan and the capitulation of U.S. Christian churches to American affluence. May its compelling biblical and evangelical critique help ignite the long struggle with justice we badly need."

—Larry Rasmussen, Reinhold Niebuhr Professor of Social Ethics, Union Theological Seminary, New York City

"I highly recommend *How Much Is Enough?* as an excellent study resource to enable Christians to learn how God wants to more fully use our lives to make a difference in a needy world."

—Tom Sine, author of *Mustard Seed vs. McWorld* and *Living on Purpose*

"Art Simon combines a pastor's heart with an activist's commitment. The result is a wise, gracious, and life-giving book that invites us into fuller expressions of Christian discipleship."

—Christine Pohl, professor of social ethics, Asbury Theological Seminary

"As a pastor Arthur Simon radiates his deep knowledge of the Gospels. As a moral leader he helps the readers of this moving book to understand the emptiness of a society based on the sterility of consumerism."

—Robert F. Drinan, S.J., professor of law, Georgetown University Law Center

"Art Simon's wisdom is precious—not just to guide us to feed the hungry, but to help us see the meaning of life even if we think we are full. His Sabbath advice is itself worth the price of the book."

—James W. Skillen, president, Center for Public Justice

"Making meaningful and challenging connections among our Christian tradition, our personal lives and our global community, Simon invites us to make the critical move in consciousness and action from personal compassion to public justice."

—Mary Ann Zollmann, BVM, president, Leadership Conference of Women Religious

"In *How Much Is Enough?* Arthur Simon has integrated a lifetime of accumulated wisdom. He combines sound biblical teaching, an array of stories and personal confessions, and a comprehensive, fresh understanding of our relationship to God and others. Even though our emphases differ at one point—his on public action, ours on the potential billions of dollars that church members could command through increased giving to help others in Jesus' name—page after page of this remarkable book provides rich and challenging insight. For example, Simon emphasizes family life and offers a roadmap to all those attempting to make sense of contemporary culture within their own homes. We recommend this book to every church member and congregation who wants to know how to be rich indeed."

—John and Sylvia Ronsvalle, empty tomb, inc.

All royalties
for the sale of this book
go to
**Bread for the World**
a U.S. Christian movement
that seeks justice for the world's hungry people
by lobbying the nation's decision makers.

For more information, contact
Bread for the World
50 F Street, N.W., Suite 500
Washington, D.C. 20001

Phone: 1-800-82-BREAD

E-mail: bread@bread.org

Web site: http://www.bread.org

# HOW MUCH IS ENOUGH?

## HUNGERING FOR GOD IN AN AFFLUENT CULTURE

## ARTHUR SIMON

Baker Books

A Division of Baker Book House Co
Grand Rapids, Michigan 49516

© 2003 by Arthur Simon

Published by Baker Books
a division of Baker Book House Company
P.O. Box 6287, Grand Rapids, MI 49516-6287
www.bakerbooks.com

Second printing, April 2003

Printed in the United States of America

Library of Congress Cataloging-in-Publication Data

Simon, Arthur R.
    How much is enough? : hungering for God in an affluent culture /
Arthur Simon.
        p.    cm.
    Includes bibliographical references.
    ISBN 0-8010-6408-2 (pbk.)
    1. Wealth—Religious aspects—Christianity.  2. Christian Life.  I.
Title.
BR115 .W4 S56  2003
241' 68—dc21                                            2002014958

To my daughter Leah,
a special gift,
a special joy.
May she become all
that God would have her be
in Jesus Christ.

# Contents

# Acknowledgments

More people have helped in various ways in the preparation of this book than can be properly acknowledged, including members of my family and various staff members at Bread for the World. I wish to thank in particular those who read my initial draft and offered suggestions that were invaluable to me in preparing the final draft. Though the flaws remain my own, this book is far better because of their advice. The readers are David Beckmann (whose idea it was that I write the book), Dorothy Drummond, Robert Gorman, John C. Haughey, S. J., David and Robin Miner, Aimee Moiso, Lloyd Neve, Harold Remus, Paul Simon, and Gerard Straub. Dolly Youssef copied the manuscript and mailed it to them, among other countless ways in which she helped. Others who provided advice, information, and encouragement along the way include Emily Byers, Kay Dowhower, Kathleen Dougherty, Shawnda Eibl, Tim Ek, Dick Hoehne, Barbara Howell, Diane Hunt, Paul Marshall, Joe Martingale, Christine Matthews, Don McClanen, Russ Melby, Barbara Miller, Andrea Moresca, Tom Murphy, Jane Remson, Barbara Rockow, Malcolm Street, Phil Strickland, and Rhodes Thompson. I am truly grateful to all of them.

11

# A Preliminary Word

A Christian from Germany visited the United States shortly after World War II. "I notice your churches have cushions," he commented, suggesting churches of affluence. Then he added, "I notice your preaching has cushions, too." He had gotten a sampling of feel-good sermons that treaded lightly (if at all) on the expectations God has for us regarding love and justice toward the poor, and in this case especially toward marginalized African Americans. The preaching he heard seemed to soothe believers—either with the idea that their lives were perfectly fine, or perhaps awful but not to worry because forgiveness is cheap.

On these pages, I try to eliminate the cushions so we hear Jesus clearly and do not continue to worship modern-day golden calves, oblivious or unconcerned with the fact that we are doing so. When that happens we miss out on joy— the joy of receiving God's extravagant grace (which does not seem so amazing if we sense little need of it), and the joy of turning our life toward its real purpose.

This book looks at both the cost and the joy of discipleship. The first seven chapters focus mainly on ways in which an affluent culture turns our hearts toward fleeting satisfactions and away from God. That is the bad news. It is necessary to face the bad news as honestly as possible, so we see how we are being snookered; but it does make for some painful reading, a bit like surgery.

The good news becomes more prominent in the latter part of the book. The bad news will, I hope, help us understand and welcome the good news more gratefully. Life is a gift from God, and God wants us to celebrate it fully. Jesus provides the way to do so.

The first chapter offers an initial snapshot of the challenge we face. Chapter 2 flags our spiritual emptiness and puts some hard words of Jesus alongside human needs. Chapter 3 tells how the early Christians found a new hope and tried to be faithful to it, often at great cost. Because we tend to blend into the culture, they serve as a different model for us. Chapter 4 deals with the "rat race" that pulls us away from the kingdom. Chapters 5–7 take a look at money, pleasure, and power—three of the most-craved idols.

Chapter 8 highlights a few things about our modern economy that show why following Jesus is no simple matter. Chapters 9–10 ask, "How much is enough?" They address some adverse consequences of affluent living for poverty-stricken people and suggest ways of helping to reverse those consequences, in part through simpler living.

Because simpler living is inadequate, chapter 11 picks up the powerful biblical theme of justice for the oppressed and shows how we can become their advocates. Chapters 12 through 14 describe the nourishment and celebration that characterize discipleship. A postscript offers a handful of practical steps that readers might want to consider.

The book can be read in one sitting, but chapters are divided into short sections for those who prefer stand-alone reflections.

Their attraction to Jesus prompted the disciples to leave everything and follow him. In the same way, Jesus invites us to a fuller, more adventurous life than we could possibly have without him. The way of the cross, yes. But beyond it the crown.

14

ONE

# That Seductive Urge

Urgently, incessantly, Jesus drew people to God. Seek first the kingdom and righteousness of God, he said (Matt. 6:33). For this we were made. Nothing else satisfies the longing of the heart. Nothing but the source of joy can give us joy. So Jesus invites us to follow him, to hunger and thirst for God, and to feast on the goodness that comes from God alone.

The other side of that coin is that anything loved and trusted more than God is certain to fail. For this reason, Jesus repeatedly warned against the seductive power of possessions, knowing that the desire for them can take us captive and separate us from God. *Mammon*,[1] he called them. "You cannot serve God and mammon" (Matt. 6:24 RSV). Jesus used the word to signify money as an object of trust, personified and worshiped. Serving mammon is a temptation in every generation, but especially our own, caught up as we are in the pursuit of affluence on an unprecedented scale.

But *how* do we serve God instead of mammon?

15

"Follow me," Jesus said. This book reflects my own struggle to do so. I hope it engages you as well, for we face the supremely difficult challenge of living faithfully for Christ in a culture that is more alien to our faith than we may realize. If our particular culture encouraged the persecution of Christians, the challenge would be more sharply drawn. But this culture doesn't beat up on most of us; it seduces us with a desire to have more of what money can buy.

This acquisitive urge often drives us to overburden ourselves—first to earn more money, and then to reap its benefits. Life gets hectic. Parents, for example, find themselves unable to give their children the time and personal attention they need. Far from delivering inner peace, living this way militates against it, leaving us instead with a gnawing discontent.

The things we want are not necessarily bad. On the contrary, many of them are stunningly good—like the computer on which I am typing this. All of us are beneficiaries of technological advances that have extended life expectancy, given us better health, better homes, better clothes, and access to information, communication, and transportation that would have been unthinkable less than a century ago. These advances have rescued vast numbers of people throughout the world—ourselves very likely included —from what otherwise would have been lives of poverty, poor health, and early death.

So what's the problem?

The problem is that the desire to have more of the things we want is addictive. It can begin to define life and its aspirations, and soon take control. The good life is seen as a life of prosperity, an essential part of the American dream. *But life so defined is hostile to the way of Jesus,* who said, "It is easier for a camel to go through the eye of a needle than for the rich to enter the kingdom of God" (Luke 18:25). That is the problem.

"But I am not rich," you may instinctively reply; and you have a point if, like me, you belong to one of the middle-income brackets that include most of us in the industrial-ized North. Compared to 99 percent of history's human population, however, or even compared to the vast majority of people in the world today, we are rich indeed. In any case, none of us has to be wealthy to covet wealth. It is the *love* of wealth, not the *amount* of wealth that starves the soul, and our culture fosters that love.

The word *culture* is rooted in the Latin word *cultus*—a system of religious worship. Culture is the way of life that grows out of the beliefs and values of a people—not nec-essarily the ones they profess to have, but the ones they really do have. A culture, then, reflects what dominates the hearts of people, what most of them love and trust and live for, and what they try to accomplish. A materialistic culture is one that by definition has emerged from the wor-ship of wealth and pursuits related to wealth. That is not the whole story of our culture, to be sure, but it is a large part of it.

I learned something of this as a boy, because my father frequently reminded us—in stories, family devotions, and conversation—of the competition between God and mam-mon for our loyalty. Later in life, two turning points riveted my mind on these lessons. The first was an invitation in 1961 to serve as pastor of a Lutheran church in New York City. The Lower East Side of Manhattan was bursting with a population from waves of earlier immigrations, along with new arrivals from Puerto Rico and the rural South. Like most others, I lived in an old tenement. Poverty was rife and families frequently ran out of food toward the end of the month, even with government assistance. The contrast between the Lower East Side and places in which I had spent the previous thirty years of my life was stark. I was struck by the obstacles that seemed to mire people in poverty and our inability as a society to find solutions.

17

The second turning point emerged from the first more than a decade later with the founding of Bread for the World as a Christian citizens' lobby. The purpose of its founding was to persuade people within the churches to let their faith be active in the work of advocating justice on behalf of hungry people. That idea took hold, and leading it occupied me for two more decades, enabling me to witness hunger and deprivation firsthand in other countries. The contrast between American abundance and the poverty I saw gave me anguish, because I sensed a connection between empty stomachs on one continent and empty lives on another.

During these years, I struggled with my own commitments and spending habits, seeking fidelity to Christ. In surroundings that impose false aspirations on all of us, I continue to struggle, learning as I go. I am guided by some clear signals from the Bible but not a full slate of answers. The witness of saints through the ages also gives me a general sense of direction, though few specific directives for the tangled web of daily decisions. In short, God points the way, but provides no paved road through the wilderness.

Each follower of Jesus faces this challenge. There are no shortcuts, no quick fixes, no "one-size-fits-all" when it comes to living as a faithful disciple. Decisions about the use of money and use of our lives more often involve shades of gray than sharp contrasts between black and white, but because those decisions make a huge difference to our own well-being and that of others, they are of immense importance. They usually involve many small steps rather than great heroic leaps. Because the results are always flawed and our motives inescapably mixed, we live by forgiveness.

To serve mammon is to turn away from God. To serve God is to reject mammon and become recipients of a totally unmerited love, a love that enables us to let go of anything to which we are captive and follow Christ.

# Fat Wallets, Empty Lives

Why is it that in the face of unprecedented prosperity, so many of us feel discontented? This is especially evident in rich countries, but it is also true in poor countries among those who have managed to attain some measure of affluence. Everywhere it is clear that material advantages can capture the heart. What they cannot do is nourish the soul.

Listen to Gerard Straub, network TV producer, explain why he abandoned his lucrative career:

> The joys I've experienced in life have all been lined with sadness. . . . All around me, I see people fighting to suppress the sadness by searching for joy in a wide array of ways: sex, power, fame, fortune, drugs. We crowd into gigantic malls and gobble up all the goodies on display. We consume more than we need because we think we need more than we have. . . . But the sadness remains.[1]

Our culture spreads before us a dazzling array of things to buy and things to do. This causes most people to experience an ever-rising level of expectations. Rising expectations expand our perception of what we need. We see things and want them, and before long we *need* them. Our expectations expand partly because new or improved products and services—many of them quite useful—become available, and partly because people around us are buying them.

Advertising plays a big role. We are "conditioned to be dissatisfied cravers rather than appreciators of the goods of the earth," writes John Cavanaugh.[2] The craving is cultivated by marketers who persuade people to buy. Today the U.S. marketing industry alone spends several times as much money as the total income of the poorest billion people on earth. Their abject poverty stands in striking contrast to the growing affluence in rich countries.

Loevi Keidel, Mennonite missionary in the Congo, returned to the States on his first furlough in 1955. He noticed that the new status symbols were a black-and-white television and wall-to-wall carpeting in the living room. On the second furlough, it was color TV and automatic washers and dryers. On the third, dishwashers and stereo sound systems. On the fourth, recreation vehicles and backyard swimming pools. On the fifth, video cameras, satellite dishes, and personal computers.[3]

The specifics vary from person to person, but expectations, like flooding waters, keep rising. To keep up, we work longer hours (on average) to lift household income. Yet, after a decade of increased incomes, polls showed that most Americans felt they were not benefiting from their nation's economic growth. Many, of course, were not. Others found that income gains were offset by harried lives and less time with family. But the feeling of standing in place also reflects constantly rising expectations—like seeing people stand in front of you at a football game, so you stand too. You use your tiptoes to gain an advantage, but the people in front of you do the same. All that rising, yet no better view.

Frantic lives and rising expectations are not the only reasons for our discontent. Consider the flaunting of coarsened sex, violence, and language in the media and in real life. There is a huge market for these, and in exploiting it people not only make money, but shape the culture. We have defined deviancy downward—lowered the bar on what passes for acceptable behavior—and this impacts our lives in the form of crime, divorce, disdain for authority, and much more. So people wonder if this is the price we pay for prosperity. Is moral decay an inevitable outcome?

Behind this culture of mammon lies a widespread myth that God and life in God are nice but largely irrelevant— mere superstition to some, for others a bit of religion we tack on to the rest of life. The natural world, on the other hand, is real. What matters in life is what we can get and enjoy for ourselves. *Our* success, *our* pleasure, *our* happiness—*we humans* are the measure of all things.

Most of us would be appalled to have this designated as our creed, and it probably is not. Yet in large decisions that may already provide the framework for our lives, such as where we reside and work, and in a host of smaller choices we make each day, we may find ourselves living by it unaware. Why? Because this creed perfectly fits our natural disposition to selfishness, and because it is part of what our surroundings offer us and impose on us as the way life is supposed to be. I am influenced by it. All of us are. The problem is not that we've tried faith and found it wanting, but that we've tried mammon and found it addictive, and as a result find following Christ inconvenient.

Centuries before Christ, one of the great Hebrew prophets also spoke to a people who had abandoned the God of the covenant for the gods of mammon and, as a result, were driven into exile: "Why spend money on what is not bread, and your labor on what does not satisfy?" (Isa. 55:2 NIV).

Why, he asked, should you do so, when God is offering you something infinitely better at no cost?

Why, indeed?

## Two Paths

A television documentary "Affluenza" begins, like a soap opera, with background organ music. A doctor is examining a woman whose symptoms include a terrible emptiness that hasn't been relieved by a new car, a new house, a boat, or a recent raise. As the organ music swells, the doctor announces: "Affluenza!"

After this mock opening, psychologist Jessie O'Neill, once a victim of runaway materialism who now specializes in its treatment, tells viewers that affluenza can make a factory worker spend a chunk of every paycheck on the lottery, a corporate executive see little of his family in order to earn eight million dollars instead of seven million dollars a year, a secretary use food money on fashion sales, or a teenager steal for a pair of sneakers. Affluenza can also show up in more subtle ways:

- Having little life outside of work
- Being preoccupied with your external appearance
- Feeling unfulfilled despite having many things
- Imagining that a new outfit, another vacation, or renovating the house will make you happy

In truth, none of us is immune to the seduction of trying to slake what is really a spiritual thirst with things that money can buy, though doing so is like drinking salt water from the sea. It turns immediate gratification into a life-threatening condition.

A far different path is the life of faith. To believe in Jesus is to trust him as Savior and follow him as Lord. That puts us on a quest entirely different than that of acquiring things, because Jesus wants to transform our purpose in life from one of getting to one of giving. When that happens, material possessions take on a new meaning. Paradoxically, they mean less and more at the same time. They mean less because they no longer have a possessive hold on us, and are no longer seen as necessary to satisfy our heart's desire. But they also mean more, because the eyes of faith, seeing their true value, can honor them as blessings entrusted to us by their rightful owner, who wants them to be used in ways that accomplish his purposes.

Following Jesus places us sharply at odds with prevailing values. Because moving against the cultural stream takes courage as well as love, we need all the help we can get. God's Word, a community of faith, and prayer are indispensable sources of strength, strongholds to anchor us against the current.

It may seem strange to expect help from the Bible, since the life of people during the various biblical eras differed so strikingly from our own. The encouragement we need most, however, is the encouragement of faith, and for that the Bible is our foundational guide. In addition, the Bible gives surprisingly clear words regarding possessions. The prophet Amos, for example, was a lowly herdsman who saw widespread greed, cheating, and trampling of the poor. The result was luxury and ease for some, but destitution for others. So when "the LORD roars from Zion" at Israel because of this (Amos 1:2 NIV), we can hear the Lord roaring at us today. The words of Amos speak eloquently of the justice God requires, even though we must apply them to more complex circumstances.

The Bible shows us not only the way to heaven, but our purpose on earth as well. It urges us to grasp two things: first, faith in Jesus as the one who rescues us from sin and death; and second, the faithful life that follows. We are driven to ask if faith, for us, is merely a security blanket for a self-seeking life or radical trust in the God who cares about us so passionately that, in Christ, he has suffered humiliation and death to reclaim us as his children. To affirm the latter is to accept transformation of our life and our values as part of God's design for us.

That puts us on a very different path.

## The Snare of Wealth

"It may be possible to have a good debate over whether or not Jesus believed in fairies," G. K. Chesterton said. "Alas, it is impossible to have any sort of debate over whether or not Jesus believed that rich people were in big trouble—there is too much evidence on the subject and it is overwhelming."[4] Jesus' strong identification with poor and socially despised people is equally beyond dispute.

"[God] has filled the hungry with good things but has sent the rich away empty," says Mary, anticipating the birth of Jesus (Luke 1:53). The Gospel of Luke reports that Jesus began his public ministry in the synagogue of Nazareth by reading from the prophet Isaiah:

> "The Spirit of the Lord is on me,
>     because he has anointed me
>     to proclaim good news to the poor.
> He has sent me to proclaim freedom for the prisoners
>     and recovery of sight for the blind,
> to release the oppressed,
>     to proclaim the year of the Lord's favor."

**LUKE 4:18-19**

Jesus then scandalized the congregation by saying, "Today this Scripture is fulfilled in your hearing" (v. 21). He not only implied that he was this Messiah, but characterized his mission as wonderful news for those who by reason of poverty,

24

servitude, physical disability, or some other oppression were widely looked down on by the devout.

Born in a stable or cave, Jesus lived simply, first as a carpenter's son, then as an itinerant prophet. "Foxes have holes and birds of the air have nests, but the Son of Man has no place to lay his head," he observed (Luke 9:58).

In Luke's version of the Beatitudes, Jesus blesses those who are poor and hungry, then adds this blunt warning:

> But woe to you who are rich,
>     for you have already received your comfort.
> Woe to you who are well fed now,
>     for you will go hungry.
>
> LUKE 6:24–25

Jesus told parables about the rich. One man, after building bigger barns for his bumper crops, congratulated himself by deciding to take it easy and enjoy his wealth; but God said, "You fool! This very night your life will be demanded from you" (Luke 12:20). Another who lived in luxury ignored the beggar Lazarus at his doorstep and ended up in eternal torment, while Lazarus was carried by the angels to be with Abraham (Luke 16:19–31). This subversive teaching overturned the prevailing notion that those who prospered had God's favor and were the ones destined to join Abraham.

Jesus depicted the final judgment as a day in which he will welcome into the kingdom those who fed the hungry, clothed the naked, and visited the sick and the imprisoned. To the astonishment of the righteous, he tells them that in doing so they had fed and clothed *him*. The rest, he said, will be self-condemned for having turned away from him (Matt. 25:31–46).

"Sell your possessions and give to the poor," Jesus told his disciples (Luke 12:33). He repeated this injunction to others as well. A young synagogue leader once approached Jesus and asked, "What must I do to inherit eternal life?"

(Luke 18:18). Jesus reminded him of the commandments. The man replied that he had kept all of them from his youth on. Jesus told him, "You still lack one thing. Sell everything you have and give to the poor, and you will have treasure in heaven. Then come, follow me" (v. 22). When he heard this, the man was deeply saddened because he had great wealth (v. 23).

In proclaiming the kingdom of God, Jesus had more to say about possessions than almost any other issue. But even this brief sampling makes us squirm, for Jesus is clearly asking for much more than we are willing to give. We are not so different from the rich young man after all.

What does this mean for us? What are we to do? To follow Jesus must we sell everything and give the proceeds to the poor? But that does not seem possible for most of us, with a job to tend, a family to support and care for, children who require an education, and other responsibilities. Life is complicated. How, then, do we deal with these words of Jesus?

We are tempted to shrug them off as unrealistic, not meant to be taken seriously. But that is the one thing we should not do. Jesus is dead serious about the snare of wealth. He wants to shake us to the core. He is ringing the alarm, saying, "Wake up, or your possessions will destroy you! Life is about something far better and more lasting!" He is also delivering the unsettling reminder that what we have is not really ours. It belongs to God. So he asks us to let go of it and "follow me."

## Hunger and Poverty

When does money become mammon? "It becomes mammon whenever our passion for nice things is stronger than our compassion for the wounded in our world," write Don McClanen and Dale Stitt.[5]

When Jesus saw people who were wounded, his heart went out to them. Those physically or spiritually ill were not problems to him, but persons he deeply loved. The hungry and the poor were never abstract statistics, but always people close to the heart of God. Statistics, of course, can help to inform us about hunger and poverty, but in the end we need to see not numbers and categories, but people. And not stereotypes, either, particularly those that demean poor people and view poverty as a sign of moral failure—and by implication our own status above poverty as moral superiority. No, to see hunger and poverty is to see real human beings.

I saw a bit of poverty as a child during the Depression. Strangers often knocked at the door of our house to ask for food. Some poor families belonged to our church and one of them lost a fourteen-year-old son when he was struck by a car while riding a bicycle. I vividly remember old Mr. Smith, the father, sobbing inconsolably at the graveside when Emil was buried, and weeping with grief myself because of his grief. Poverty did not diminish even slightly the love they had for one another or the family's anguish when Emil died.

Our family was not exactly well-to-do. My father drew a spartan salary as a Lutheran pastor in Eugene, Oregon. The parsonage, as we called it, was an old, small farmhouse around which the town had grown. Some of our members were farmers and brought us produce, mostly fruits and vegetables that my mother would can for later use. We had little to spare, but we didn't go hungry, either, and because so many were much worse off, it never occurred to me to think of ourselves as poor. For the most part, I was sheltered from real poverty, saw little of it, and seldom thought about it.

While attending seminary and helping my brother Paul in his initial campaign for public office, I once canvassed maybe a hundred families living in rickety shacks in an isolated area called "the island" in Venice, Illinois, across the Mississippi River from St. Louis. This sobering experience gave me a glimpse of life for some of the poorest descendants of American slaves, and I wondered about the absence of the church—at least *my* church and most churches—from the lives of these people. I wondered about my own absence, as well, and how, in the face of such neglect by us, they could be expected to trust in God.

Years later, in a poverty-scarred section of New York, I reflected on these earlier observations of poor people. But now I was living among them, seeing their struggles, joys, and sorrows up close: a mother raising her children in hostile surroundings, a child whose eyes danced with promise, a teenager turning to sex and drugs, a family trusting God despite constant hardships.

To know people, of course, is not to romanticize them, but to know also their weaknesses—think of your own family or yourself, for example. This applies to the poor, as well. To see them as people is to sense how human, how much like ourselves they are, and so to feel more deeply the pain of their poverty. Their need and the love of God can intersect in our hearts.

That intersection is the key to the witness of Moses and the prophets and of Jesus himself regarding poor and hungry people. It explains, at least in part, their warnings about the danger of wealth: the capacity of its pursuit and enjoyment to pull people away from God and from others, and to do so especially at the expense of the most vulnerable. Those warnings remind us that choices we make regarding our use of wealth, however modest that wealth may be, often determine whether others eat or go hungry, live or die. We can lavish our bit of bounty upon ourselves, or we can share it with others.

> Suppose a brother or sister is without clothes and daily food. If one of you says to them, "Go in peace; keep warm and well fed," but does nothing about their physical needs, what good is it? In the same way, faith by itself, if it is not accompanied by action, is dead.
>
> **JAMES 2:15–17**

28

There is misery, says Richard Foster, when people *lack* provision; but there is also misery when they try to make a *life* out of provision.[6]

## Control of the Heart

Money and its use are matters of the soul, because they cannot be separated from the question of where our ultimate commitment lies. What do we love above all else? Where do we place our trust? What or whom do we therefore worship? According to Jesus, money entices us to idolatry for the simple reason that, under the guise of giving us what we want, it seeks control.

The case of the rich young synagogue official (Luke 18:18–30) is instructive. Jesus did not tell everyone he met, even every rich person, to sell all their possessions and give to the poor. Shortly after his encounter with the rich young man, Jesus visited Zacchaeus the tax collector (Luke 19:1–10). When Zacchaeus told Jesus that he was going to make fourfold restitution to those he had defrauded and give half of his possessions to the poor, Jesus did not say, "What about the other half?" Rather, he exclaimed, "Today salvation has come to this house!" But the rich young man is singled out and asked to sell everything. Why? Not because Jesus wanted the man's money, but because he wanted his *heart*. "Jesus looked at him and *loved* him," notes the Gospel of Mark (Mark 10:21). Jesus perceived that the man was in love with his wealth, that his riches controlled his heart. So Jesus asked him to give up the power that held him captive.

Jesus also needed to break the man's shell of confidence in having faithfully kept all the commandments from his youth, because in his obedience to the law he had missed the *essence* of the law: to love God with your whole heart, soul, and mind; and to love your neighbor as yourself. With one simple invitation, Jesus stripped away the man's righ-

29

teous facade and let him see himself as a wayward soul, incapable of doing what God required. Possessions controlled him. Consequently, he went away sorrowful. Sorrowful, as in full of sorrow, but empty of heart.

The exchange between this young man and Jesus prompted Jesus to tell his disciples, "It is easier for a camel to go through the eye of a needle than for the rich to enter the kingdom of God" (Luke 18:25). The disciples realized that the statement placed them and everyone else in jeopardy; so in astonishment they asked, "Who then can be saved?" (v. 26). ("If it's that difficult, how can any of us make it?") Jesus replied, "What is humanly impossible is possible with God."

And there lies our hope.

# THREE

# Hope and Purpose

"The Christian life comes not by gritting our teeth but by falling in love," writes Richard Foster.[1]

Jesus' words about possessions, and his call to deny self, take up the cross, and follow him (Mark 8:34), sound a lot like an invitation to grit your teeth. But they seem to have had the opposite effect on his followers. Jesus' death and resurrection, along with the gift of the Holy Spirit, gave them a hope and a purpose that fired their lives as they began forming a new community of faith. They clearly had fallen in love with God for having loved them so lavishly in Christ.

The response of these believers to the teaching of Jesus about possessions illustrates this exceptionally well, for as their movement expanded, believers displayed a keen awareness of attachment to mammon as idolatry and generosity to the poor as a service to God. But they practiced these commitments in ways that varied.

The most dramatic example of continuity with Jesus' teachings came in and around Jerusalem after Pentecost.

Believers devoted themselves daily, in the temple and in their homes, to the apostles' teaching, fellowship, the breaking of bread, and prayer. Healings by the apostles added to the excitement that the Jesus movement created. In addition, "All the believers were together and had everything in common. They sold property and possessions to give to anyone who had need" (Acts 2:44–45). This powerful expression of faith drew widespread admiration from people and contributed to the fact that "the Lord added to their number daily those who were being saved" (v. 47). Official opposition, including the arrest of Peter and John, only generated more zeal.

> All the believers were one in heart and mind. No one claimed that any of their possessions was their own, but they shared everything they had. With great power the apostles continued to testify to the resurrection of the Lord Jesus. And God's grace was so powerfully at work in them all that there were no needy persons among them. For from time to time those who owned lands or houses sold them, brought the money from the sales and put it at the apostles' feet, and it was distributed to anyone who had need.
>
> ACTS 4:32–35

These followers of Jesus showed a remarkable commitment to him, especially in view of the instructions in the Hebrew Bible for keeping property in the family. Responding to Jesus in this way was almost surely related to their expectation that the Lord would return in the very near future. Before long, however, famine and dire poverty gripped Judea, prompting the apostle Paul to go to great lengths to gather a collection, mostly from the largely Gentile churches in Asia Minor, for the stricken Christians in Judea (Gal. 2:10; 2 Cor. 8–9).

Was Jesus' instruction to sell and share possessions intended for all believers? Was it a specialized calling for a smaller circle of disciples? Like the woman's pouring of expensive ointment on Jesus' feet before his crucifixion, was the action of the Christians in Jerusalem a monumental expression of love intended for some Christians in every age, but not for universal replication in the church?

The practice in Jerusalem was voluntary and does not seem to have been expected or attempted elsewhere as young churches sprang up throughout the Roman empire. However, the drumbeat of warnings against attachment to wealth, along with admonitions to share generously with the poor, emerge repeatedly from the New Testament's record of life in the early church and are evident in the care early Christians gave not only to their own, but to others as well. Jesus' teachings clearly helped shape the faith of these believers. From the evidence we have, they responded in ways that made a profound impact on others. But that did not include a requirement that converts sell their possessions, as a letter addressed to Paul's protégé Timothy indicates:

> Command those who are rich in this present world not to be arrogant nor to put their hope in wealth, which is so uncertain, but to put their hope in God . . . [and] to do good, to be rich in good deeds, and to be generous and willing to share.

> 1 TIMOTHY 6:17–18

Such an instruction and others like it reflect the presence of rich Christians in the early church. Though apparently a tiny minority, some, like Philemon, made their homes available to fellow believers as houses of worship and hospitality.

What do we learn from this? Do we give a sigh of relief that Jesus is letting us off the hook? Hardly. Rather we should note how eagerly these early Christians accepted the work and words of Jesus, and how diligently they practiced them in application to their own varied circumstances.

Not perfectly, to be sure, but well enough to shake the world. They did so because they had found a great hope and a new purpose in Christ.

I thought of them when the morning newspaper featured Rob Marsh, a physician decorated for rescue efforts, despite near-fatal wounds, in Somalia. The son of a former secretary of the U.S. Army, Marsh moved with his wife and (now four) young children to an area of rural Virginia that had no physician instead of pursuing a lucrative practice. "He goes where the need is greatest," said a colleague. An elder in his Presbyterian church, he travels over gravel roads in a pickup truck to make house calls and refuses to send his patients bills. But they are not just patients to Marsh. He considers them friends, so he gets involved in all aspects of their lives. "I feel that's why I was saved, to come back here and do this," says Marsh. "This is my calling."[2]

## A New Identity

The early Christians knew who they were. They stood out among their peers for professing that a young Jewish rabbi executed in Jerusalem was the Son of God, crucified to atone for human sinfulness but risen from the dead. They believed that through the sacred rite of baptism they had *already* died to sin with Christ and risen with him to a new and eternal life (Rom. 6:1–11). Jesus now *was* their life—the great treasure buried in a field, in return for which one would give up all other possessions (Matt. 13:44).

The starting place for the early Christians, however, was not the question: What do I need to give up to follow Jesus? The starting place—for them and for us—was the good news of Jesus' victory and the question he asked his disciples, "Who do you say I am?" (Mark 8:29). By discovering Jesus, they discovered themselves.

Those early Jewish and Gentile converts heard the good news from very different vantage points. Jews had knowledge of the God who created all things, and of being included in a special covenant God had made with their ancestors, once slaves in Egypt and exiles in Babylon. They had familiarity with the prophets who promised deliverance from oppression. In Palestine, messianic hopes were widespread and sometimes intense during the time of Jesus. As the Gospels and other early sources indicate, these had a distinctly political and sometimes militant orientation.

Gentiles, on the other hand, were surrounded by more gods than they could keep track of, including the most official god, the emperor himself. All of this was of little help in giving people a defining purpose in life.

Jesus offered both Jews and Gentiles a new identity as children of God through the gift of forgiveness. That new identity was sealed by God when they were baptized. Baptism meant freedom, but nothing like the modern illusion of autonomous freedom. Rather, it freed them from the grip of mammon and other captivities to become captive to Christ. The apostle Paul put it this way: "You are not your own; you were bought at a price" (1 Cor. 6:19–20). They received this lordship of Jesus not as a burden, however, but as an extraordinary gift. And belonging to Christ meant they were free to love and serve others (Gal. 5:13–14).

Their new status gave them a transcendent purpose— that of living to the glory of God. To live for self is to put self in the center of things, where God alone belongs. Doing so is revolt against the source of our being. It is the path of alienation. We have been created and redeemed to live for God and to love one another.

For those early Christians, belonging to Christ also meant becoming an intimate part of a *community* of believers, the new visible presence of Christ in the world. "The body of Christ," Paul called it. In this community, faith was shared and nourished, the bread and wine of Christ's body and blood received, and prayer and praise lifted up to God. It was a community of love that prepared believers to be faithful

35

representatives of Christ in their homes and places of work, and in all other surroundings.

These early Christians remind us that only within this new life under the grace of God can we truly follow Jesus. Only his gracious love can open our hearts to share fully with others all that God has given us.

Equivocation about who we are, wavering loyalty, and accommodation to the surrounding culture may account for a deep disquiet within us. How do we deal with our soul's distress? The way to start is the way each of us must begin again each day: by remembering who we are. We do that by remembering *whose* we are, and in remembering, we are empowered to follow Christ. What does it mean for me, in the circumstances of my life, to live for the Son of God who loved me and gave himself for me? How should I take up the cross and follow him? In what ways can I lose my life for his sake? I, for one, need to ask these questions daily because I easily forget that I have been baptized into Christ.

## Earthly Pilgrims

In following Christ, we become increasingly aware that the culture in which we live is not our permanent home. God has given us an eternal hope, a purpose that both transcends and gives new meaning to this life, a vision that includes—but reaches beyond—the present scene. We are "strangers and pilgrims" on earth, "in but not of the world," a biblical theme that may strike us in very different ways, depending upon our circumstances. I tend to feel too much at home when things are going well, but when they are not, I am more apt to remember that I am merely a sojourner here and long for a heavenly city.

We have dual citizenship, one on earth and one in heaven. But our citizenship in heaven governs our earthly citizenship, which is why believers have so often been viewed as a threat to the state. In our culture believers are more likely seen as a bit odd for not celebrating the dominance of materialism.

Hope in the resurrection has been one of the great strengths of the Christian movement, as well as a great weakness. Its strength lies in the way it has motivated and empowered people to do great good. Its weakness—*our* weakness—lies in the way it can be detached from love and reduced to a preoccupation with our own personal destiny.

It is not hard to see how the distortion can develop. When asked, "Why did Jesus die for us?" children are often taught to reply, "So we can go to heaven." The teaching is accurate as far as it goes, but if it goes no further it does grave injustice to the gospel, which is reduced to a kind of afterlife insurance policy. Carried to its logical conclusion, it shows up as a form of Christianity in which the saving of my soul (and perhaps other souls) for heaven is the only matter of consequence. Works of mercy and justice are at best a sideshow, and the transitory world not worth tending to—except for my piece of it. But this otherworldly faith is, in fact, disguised worldliness, because it cherishes affluence for oneself while caring little about the suffering of others.

Being rescued from sin and death by God's work in Christ is only *half* of the good news. The other half is that we have been rescued for the earthly purpose of living for him in a life of praise to God and service to others. "He died for all, that those who live should no longer live for themselves but for him who died for them and was raised again," said Paul (2 Cor. 5:15). The letter to the Ephesians tells us that "it is by grace you have been saved, through faith—and this is not from yourselves, it is the gift of God—not by works, so that no one can boast" (2:8–9), a verse often committed to memory. But the words that follow are usually ignored: "For we are God's handiwork, *created in Christ Jesus to do good works*, which God prepared in advance for us to do" (2:10, emphasis added). We are not saved *by* good works, but *for* good works. In pointing to this purpose of grace, Paul simply echoes the words of Jesus that our good deeds are to shine so brightly before others that they will give praise to the Father in heaven (Matt. 5:16).

The resurrection empowers us for such a life. It gives us the will to take up the cross and follow Jesus, risking ridicule and death if need be in order to carry out our part of his mission. It generates an almost brazen courage—which I, as an instinctive coward, desperately need—because we have nothing to lose if "to live is Christ and to die is gain" (Phil. 1:21). Paul implies that without hope in the resurrection, he would never have endured hardships, dangers, and imprisonments (1 Cor. 15:19, 30–32). He would have simply lived a life of comfort and ease as a respectable citizen, John Piper suspects. He adds, "What stunned me about this train of thought is that many professing Christians seem to aim at just this, and call it Christianity."[3]

People who were well situated financially and socially in Jesus' day usually resisted following him. We, the affluent of today, may also resist the idea of losing control of what we have. It is a loss that will occur in any case at the moment of death, of course. Perhaps that is why we cling to it so desperately.

The resurrection, however, gives us reason to aim much higher.

## Whole-Life Christians

From Jesus and the infant church, the picture of faith and life that emerges is far from instinctive to us modern-day, westernized Christians who are prone to separate faith from life. Faith is what we believe privately. Churchgoing is public, but that, too, is neatly tucked into a slot labeled "religion." What happens in church has little bearing on what we do the rest of the week. But this is faith turned upside down, for it has God sanctioning our way of life rather than taking charge of it.

This understanding would have been unthinkable to Jesus and to the early believers. Confessing Jesus as Lord meant turning all of life, not just some spiritual segment of it, over to him. How could it be any other way? The God who created the world set out to restore our fallen race in the person of God's fully human son. Consequently, Jesus is the pivotal point of history, and the pivotal point for each believer, as well. "If anyone is in Christ, there is a new creation" (2 Cor. 5:17), Paul said. As a result, we no longer regard people or things apart from Christ, but through the heart and mind of Christ. I don't do this well or consistently, but when I try, it changes the way I relate to others.

To see others apart from Christ is to disdain some, manipulate others, and think of people in terms of their value to us. But to see them as Christ sees them is to recognize them as deeply loved children of God, people for whom Christ died and for whom he has high hopes and aspirations.

We are called to see creation through the eyes of God, as an awesome miracle unfolding before our eyes. We can see our work, even its onerous aspects, as a way of contributing to the well-being of others, while seeking justice and improvement in the workplace. We can seek the common good through works of mercy and peace, doing our part in community affairs, and taking responsibility as citizens to help achieve public justice through the instruments of government.

We can be salt and light in the world, enriching and ennobling the culture, when others are dragging it down. We can see the countless gifts and blessings poured upon us each day, and lift our hearts in continual thanksgiving. We can pray for others and seize opportunities to act in love toward those who are as near to us as our own family and as far away as foreign lands.

We can be God's stewards, taking care of the earth for its owner. My morning newspaper features high-tech fishing that is depleting the ocean of fish and depriving small-scale fishermen of a livelihood—just one example of greed that makes us act more like hijackers than stewards. "We are treating our planet in an inhuman and god-forsaken manner because we see things in an inhuman, god-forsaken way. And we see things in this way because that is basically how we see ourselves," writes Eastern Orthodox theologian Philip Sherrard.[4] Perhaps we see ourselves that way because we tend to become like whatever we love and trust the most, and in trusting the products of our hand, we become less human. For the same reason, we may see other people as inhuman and god-forsaken, and therefore worthy of neglect.

Unfortunately, the word *stewardship* has been monopolized in Protestant circles by those who have responsibility for raising money to support the church. "Stewardship Sunday" is the day for making annual pledges in many churches, and when stewardship is the sermon topic, parishioners know very well what the bottom line will be, despite obligatory references to time and talent. "Brainwashed from pulpit and pew, stewardship has traded its vocation of serving the world for a preoccupation with saving the church," writes Rhodes Thompson.[5] But in truth, our stewardship involves the whole of life—anything and everything that has been entrusted to us.

Even the word *treasure* gets shortchanged. Tithing is frequently pitched as ideal stewardship. One hesitates to question tithing, since tithers are *way* above average in church giving. Tithing, however, may imply that the other 90 percent is off-limits to stewardship, and that if God gets 10 percent, the rest is *ours*. The point is not that God should get a higher take, say 30 or even 90 percent. The point is that God should get it *all*. All of it—and all of life—belongs to God. We have simply been entrusted to use everything in the best, most loving, and wisest way possible for the purposes of God. What if Jesus had asked Zacchaeus to tithe? Jesus would have been asking for a small piece of the tax collector's wealth rather than for his life. Instead, he invited a far more generous outpouring of love by helping Zacchaeus mend his broken covenant with God and experience God's grace.[6]

## Compassion for Others

The purpose of every believer's life is to glorify God. Our living for Christ is expressed in prayer and praise, in fellowship with other believers, and in our nourishment from Word and sacrament. Neglect these and we stunt our growth, waste away spiritually, and risk death of soul.

At the same time, the presence of God in prayer and worship is connected by the prophets to lives of compassion for the poor (Isa. 58:3–10). Without that connection, we pray and fast in vain. The apostle Paul expressed alarm about Christians in Corinth who, in celebrating the Lord's Supper, stuck to customary class distinctions and ate and drank beyond enough, while their poorer brothers and sisters went hungry (1 Cor. 11:17–34)—a remarkable snapshot of our world today. They were "sinning against the body and blood of the Lord," Paul wrote, and by failing to respect fellow believers as part of the body of Christ, inviting judgment on themselves (v. 27).

This connection between worship and compassion underscores the fact that most of the time the way we follow Christ is by serving others. God's intention in this regard was clear from the beginning.

"Where is your brother Abel?" the Lord asked Cain (Gen. 4:9 NIV). Cain responded with a question of his own: "Am I my brother's keeper?" The Lord made clear that he was—and that *we* are.

The first few of the Ten Commandments concern our relationship with God, the rest with obligations toward family and others. With striking insight, Jesus summarized the law by elevating love for neighbor to a place right beside love for God (Matt. 22:37–40). The two are not the same,

41

but they cannot be separated, either. Though God wants our undivided loyalty, we express it primarily by doing good for those who need us, beginning in our own home.

There is, however, a special biblical emphasis on compassion toward the weakest and most vulnerable. The law of Moses commanded this, singling out widows, orphans, immigrants, and the poor. The prophets warned that God despised the prayers and burnt offerings of people who took advantage of the poor and enriched themselves at the expense of others (Amos 5:10–24). They also promised that blessing would follow justice and mercy.

> Is not this the kind of fasting I have chosen:
>      to loose the chains of injustice . . .
>      to set the oppressed free . . . ?
> Is it not to share your food with the hungry
>      and to provide the poor wanderer with shelter—
>      when you see the naked, to clothe him . . . ?
> Then your light will break forth like the dawn,
>      and your healing will quickly appear. . . .

**ISAIAH 58:6–8 NIV**

Jesus urged sacrificial generosity to the poor. Support for the synagogue and temple is implicit in the Gospels, but the parable of the despised Samaritan (Luke 10:30–37) suggests that churchly service (represented by the priest and Levite who passed by) is no substitute for helping people in dire need.

Two friends of mine from college days know what this means. Ray and Nancy Johnsen had two healthy children when Nancy gave birth to Jimmy, a boy with multiple handicaps. Advised first to abort him and later to have him placed in an institution, Ray and Nancy instead received Jimmy as a gift from God. Knowing the enormous effort it would entail, they gave Jimmy all the affection and help he needed to be a happy boy and become a gainfully employed adult. Sacrifice? Nancy simply says, "Jim is a precious young man. He has been a great blessing and inspiration to us and we love him so very much."

Needs surround us in every family and every neighborhood. Some of the most affluent communities are rife with emotional and spiritual poverty, children in need of love and guidance rather than toys and television. Elsewhere, hunger and poverty are prevalent, though usually out of our sight and out of our mind. Everywhere problems abound, begging for people of compassion to step in and help. What will we do?

Consider the desperation of people in the most poverty-stricken countries, where children are more apt to be malnourished than go to school, more apt to die in childhood than learn to read and write.

Yaguine Koita, age fourteen, and Fode Tounkara, fifteen, froze to death on a Sabena airplane somewhere between the capital of Guinea, a small West African country, and Brussels. They were so desperate to flee their impoverished homeland and get an education that they stowed away in the landing gear bay. They left behind a letter "to the excellencies and officials of Europe" that they hoped would be read in case they died. The letter, full of spelling errors, said:

> We suffer enormously in Africa. Help us. We have problems in Africa. We lack rights as children. We have war and illness, we lack food. . . . We have schools, but we lack education. . . . We want to study, and we ask you to help us to study so we can be like you, in Africa.[7]

What will we do to help, we who are so prosperous and who belong to the one who said, "Sell your possessions and give to the poor. Provide purses for yourselves that will not wear out, a treasure in heaven that will never fail. . . . For where your treasure is, there your heart will be also" (Luke 12:33–34)?

## Spiritual Hunger and Poverty

A faithful reading of the Bible leaves no doubt that God has called us to give ourselves to others, and that foremost among the "others" are those closest to us and those, such as the poor and hungry, who are most vulnerable. The same faithful reading of Scripture is equally clear that we are called to reach those who are *spiritually* starving and impoverished. There is no use imagining that we are fully engaged in loving others if we tend to their physical needs but ignore their need for God.

Many believers seem to care only about the spiritual welfare of others, paying no attention to the hardship and injustice they suffer. How sad. But many other believers seem to care only about the physical and material needs of people, completely ignoring their spiritual poverty. Such believers may deplore the worship of mammon, and at the same time imply that a little prosperity is all poor people need. The contradiction would be humorous were it not so loveless. To love others is to love them as complete persons, body and soul, not one detached from the other.

We must start with ourselves, addressing our own spiritual poverty, for we are fellow beggars of God's grace, pointing other beggars to the one who has provided for us so generously with unmerited love and forgiveness. Otherwise we witness to our pride and self-righteousness rather than to God's goodness, imagining that we are better than those who have not tasted the goodness of the Lord.

Christians are frequently wary about sharing their faith in Christ. I know I am. We are sometimes shy—even terrified—to do so, and we need the courage of the Holy Spirit to be ready to explain the reason for the hope we have. That reason can be given in simple, natural ways, without a theological degree. This does not detract from the fact that we usually express our faith best by what we do, not by what we say. The saying, however, is also essential.

Some Christians think of faith-sharing as an imposition, a kind of arrogance that fails to respect the beliefs of others. That would be so if our salvation were something we had earned. But because it comes purely from God's grace, not our own goodness, we are simply telling of a gift that God has given us. To remain silent about that gift fails to credit the giver and may suggest that our own achievement is what has given us peace with God.

Still other believers have been scared off by the glibness of Christians who push the gospel like hucksters. These embarrassing folks have made many Christians reluctant to talk about their faith because they don't want to be identi-fied with such tactics. The answer, however, is not to turn the field over to this kind of witnessing, but to share our hope in more appropriate ways. The overriding message is that except for the work of Christ we are lost, and through him is life with God. Of course we want to respect those who believe differently, and we want to approach them gra-ciously. But we can pray for opportunities to speak the truth in love, and we will find joy in talking with others about the thing all of us need most.

Debbie, a young college graduate, worked under church auspices with impoverished children in El Salvador for a year. She told me she found great satisfaction in her work, despite the hardship. Though her faith led her there, she said she did not want to impose her faith on others. Impose? No, of course not. But share? Why not? The witness of mis-sionaries and their converts through the ages enabled us to know Christ. By what logic of the kingdom should the great-est of God's gifts to us now be kept from others?

The parable that has puzzled more people than any other is instructive in this regard. It is Jesus' story of the dishonest manager (Luke 16). A rich man, Jesus said, notified the man-ager of his estate that he would be fired because of his mis-management. The man was desperate not to dig ditches or be left on the street, so he thought of a way of ingratiating

himself to others so they would come to his aid. He called
in those who were indebted to his master, and substantially
reduced the debt of each. The master commended the dishonest steward—not for his dishonesty, but for his shrewd-
ness. Jesus observed that unbelievers are more astute in
achieving their purposes than believers are in achieving
theirs. Then he drew the lesson: "I tell you, use worldly
wealth [mammon] to gain friends for yourselves, so that when
it [mammon] is gone, you will be welcomed into eternal
dwellings" (Luke 16:9). We are to use money in such a way
(a year in El Salvador?) that we point people to the love of
God in Christ and can one day experience with them the
inexpressible joy of a grand reunion in heaven. This, too, is
why Jesus has asked us to give to the poor and follow him.

## Returning Home

Our identity and our purpose in life are anchored in God.
Cut off from our anchor we are adrift, alienated from the
source of our being and therefore—it should not surprise
us—alienated from our own self and from one another. That
is why God's work in Christ is to bring us home where we
belong—at peace with God, with ourselves, and with one
another.

St. Augustine said, "Our heart is restless until it finds its
rest in You." The Bible links this hungering for God with
our physical hunger and well-being. God's own work of reconciliation is always accompanied by works of love: God's
providential care, a covenant with Israel, freedom from slavery, messengers of warning and grace (the prophets), and at
last God's coming in Jesus of Nazareth who healed the sick,
preached to the poor, welcomed the despised and rejected,
and finally laid down his life for the world.

The feeding of the multitude illuminates this connection
between physical and spiritual hunger. Jesus had compassion
on the crowd both because they were famished and because

46

they were like sheep without a shepherd. So he nourished them, body and soul, with bread and with the Good News of the kingdom. His compassion in feeding them was as much a sign of the kingdom as were his words. Jesus connected the two, but he also distinguished between them. Bread for the body and bread from heaven are not the same; so, he warned, better not set your hope on bread that perishes, but on bread that endures for eternal life (John 6:27).

We are called by Jesus to come home to the Father because he loves us deeply. Having come home, we are called to engage ourselves fully in God's work in the world, a work of compassion for people.

The parable of the prodigal son (Luke 15:11–32) tells us that home is where the Father is, that the Father is heart-broken when we are lost, that he is constantly and eagerly waiting for us to come to our senses—to give up our affection for mammon and other created things—and return to him. We may be like the prodigal son who lost his way and wasted his life. Or we may be like the older son who stuck doggedly to his responsibilities and resented the attention that his no-account brother got when he returned. I sometimes resemble one, sometimes the other. But it was ulti-mately the prodigal who discovered what home meant, for it is the extravagant love of the father that we need to experience and emulate, not the self-indulgence of the prodigal or the pinched legalism of his brother.

Jesus reached out to the prodigals of his day and was usu-ally rejected by the religiously dutiful, who were more self-righteous than righteous. Maybe, like the prodigal, we need to come home. Or maybe, like the older brother, we need to identify with the prodigal and with the father—to see the father's lavish love and our need to be lavish with our own love. That, too, is coming home.

Jesus had this homecoming in mind when he invited peo-ple to let go of their possessions, give to the poor, and follow him.

# Rushing to Nowhere

They were running hand in hand, and the Queen went
so fast that it was all [Alice] could do to keep up with her:
and still the Queen kept crying "Faster! Faster!" . . .

The most curious part of the thing was, that . . . however fast they went, they never seemed to pass
anything. . . .

"In *our* country," said Alice, . . ."you'd generally get to
somewhere else—if you ran very fast for a long time as
we've been doing."

"A slow sort of country!" said the Queen. "Now, *here*,
you see, it takes all the running you can do, to keep in
the same place. If you want to get somewhere else, you
must run at least twice as fast as that."

**LEWIS CARROLL, *THROUGH THE LOOKING GLASS*[1]**

Ours is a restless culture. Life has become excessively busy
for a large portion of the population. Stress is almost built
into our body clocks. I am not a fast driver, probably slower
than most. But sometimes I find myself hurrying to get

somewhere—switching lanes, passing traffic, going through yellow lights—when it occurs to me that the only thing putting pressure on me to rush is my own state of mind.

Stress, of course, may come from trying to help others as much as possible. Far more often it reflects a culture that pervades a thousand habits. Our wants are constantly expanding, and our income usually lags behind. More hours to work, more things to do, and more places to go create pressure. Far from producing a sense of inner peace, this style of life nurtures a spiritual void.

Almost two centuries ago, Alexis de Tocqueville observed both the restlessness and the "strange melancholy" of Americans in the midst of prosperity. Although they were paupers compared to their counterparts of today, Tocqueville said that "Americans cleave to the things of this world as if assured that they will never die, and yet are in such a rush to snatch any that come within their reach, as if expecting to stop living before they have relished them. They clutch everything but hold nothing fast, and so lose grip as they hurry after some new delight."[2]

As the twenty-first century began and the United States was about to achieve ten years of unbroken economic growth, *The New York Times* reported as "a central fact of American life" that "most of the nation's 72 million families feel they cannot make ends meet."[3] Middle-income working families were making more money than ever, but family debt and hours spent at work had also risen. What stresses them, the article said, are expenditures: new clothes, child care, lessons, eating out, movies, home decoration, big-screen television sets, computers, stereo systems, Christmas gifts, and saving for college and retirement. For these expenses, most families needed more than one income.

About the same time, a national poll of women revealed that two of their major concerns were the time crunch (more time at work, less with family) and a perceived decline in the nation's moral values. Ironically, those polled also thought

50

that the best way to reverse the decline in moral values was for parents to spend more time with their children.[4]

According to another poll, most Americans feel that new technological advances such as cell phones and the Internet give people *less* rather than more free time. Most of those surveyed say they would rather have an extra day off than an extra day's pay.[5] The new technology keeps us working more than ever but feeling like we are slipping further behind.

How much of our spending is culturally imposed and how much represents a wise and faithful investment is a question that begs for consideration. Parents, families, and groups within the church could make this question part of their walk with God. The answer is neither self-evident nor the same for everyone. But the grace of God that undergirds discipleship provides the necessary common ground. What would giving all these things to God mean? Which ones might we get rid of? Which might we think of and use in a different way?

Timothy was advised that "godliness with contentment is great gain. For we brought nothing into the world, and we can take nothing out of it. But if we have food and clothing, we will be content with that" (1 Tim. 6:6–8). It may have been easier, even better, for Christians of the first century than for their Western counterparts of the twenty-first century to draw the line at food and clothing—though for millions of people worldwide, adequate food and clothing are still beyond reach. To aspire to godliness with contentment, however, is great gain in any century.

## Putting Life in Focus

The wisdom of godliness with contentment can help us examine ourselves. What are we doing or trying to do with our lives? How are we using our time, our abilities, and our money? Self-examination is useful whether we feel overwhelmed and frantic or insufficiently engaged. If we are too busy, we probably need to cut back. The primary aim, however, should not be to do less or to spend less, but to discern what *God* wants us to do with our life and focus on doing that well. The rest follows.

Too often, in big as well as in small decisions, *we* decide what to do and ask God to tag along. This gets things backwards. In his *Spiritual Exercises*, Ignatius Loyola says that many Christians "first choose marriage which is a means and secondarily to serve God in their married state, which service to God is the end. . . . These individuals do not go straight to God but want God to come straight to their inordinate attachments. Acting thus, they make a means of the end and an end of the means so that what they ought to seek first they seek last."[6]

We frequently reduce God to an afterthought. In examining a particular activity or purchase, we can ask: What is driving us? For what purpose are we doing this activity, or getting that item? If you are like me, most of the time the questions do not even occur to you. We make decisions casually, like buying one toy at a time until the closet of life is full of unused toys. The unspoken reason, in that case, is apt to be "It will make me happier." If so, be skeptical. Happiness does not lie in the next acquisition.

Larry Burkett writes about his pursuit of economic security, which robbed him of time with family and God. One morning he came home from work, crawled into bed at 2:00 A.M. and thought about Psalm 127:2: "In vain you rise up early and stay up late, toiling for food to eat—for he grants sleep to those he loves" (NIV). Burkett decided to limit his work week to forty-eight hours and found that he accomplished more than when he had worked twice as long. He adds, "I've never met a successful businessperson who came to the end of life and said, 'I wish I had spent more time at work and had made just a little more money.'"[7]

We may feel harried, with too much to do and not enough time to do it. Yet studies reveal that most of us are making poor use of our leisure time; we are also frequently bored, and may try to buy our way out of boredom with the latest distraction. There is a certain irony in the fact that the perception of too much work and too many activities exists side by side with spending four-and-a-half hours a day watching television, the average for U.S. adults.[8] Perhaps partly because of what it is feeding our hearts and minds, and partly because it is passive entertainment, watching television gives us remarkably little satisfaction. Psychologist David G. Myers cites a study that showed only 3 percent of those watching television were fully absorbed in that diversion, while 39 percent felt apathetic. For those engaged in activities such as gardening or talking to friends the figures flipped: 47 percent were fully absorbed and 4 percent apathetic. Not knowing what to do with their free time (when they have it) or feeling too tired for active recreation, most people resort to passive leisure that tends to leave them feeling weaker, more irritable, and less happy.[9]

The baffling combination of activity-related stress and poor use of leisure adds to the evidence that burnout often stems not from doing too much, but from the impression that no matter how much we do, we are not getting anywhere. Pushed and pulled in many directions, we feel caught on a treadmill, expending a lot of energy without accomplishing much. If it also feels as though our soul is beginning to run on empty, burnout may be around the corner.

The Danish philosopher Søren Kierkegaard understood some of this more than a century and a half ago:

> To be busy is to occupy oneself, divided and scattered (which follows from the object that occupies one), with all the multiplicity in which it is simply impossible for a person to be whole. . . . To be busy is, divided and scattered, to occupy oneself with what makes a person divided and scattered. But Christian love, which is the fulfilling of the Law, is whole and collected, present in its every expression, and yet it is

sheer action; consequently it is as far from inaction as it is from busyness.[10]

"Purity of heart is to will one thing,"[11] Kierkegaard said. Paul likewise urged singleness of heart. James linked double-mindedness with instability. Jesus told us to love God with all our heart, soul, and mind, and to love others as ourselves. He also said, "Follow me." These all speak against fractured lives and in favor of focus—putting our hearts where they belong and revamping the details of life accordingly.

There is freedom from bondage in doing so.

## Our Children

Nowhere is the need to follow Christ greater or our difficulty more apparent than in the family. Shortly after helping to launch Bread for the World, I had the unexpected opportunity to visit privately with Mother Teresa for about thirty minutes. We were discussing world hunger, when she startled me by saying, "In your country you have an even bigger problem. So many of your children are starved for love and affection."

Good intentions go astray, and in wanting to give our children the best we may serve up the worst—the mammon that so easily addicts. We withhold what they need the most: ourselves and the riches of God's love. As a certified workaholic, I confess to my great shame of having shortchanged my children in this regard. For many of you, it is not too late to make a difference in the amount of time spent with your children.

When asked to name the single factor that has done more damage to families than any other, child psychologist James Dobson replied:

It would be the almost universal condition of fatigue and time pressure, which leaves every member of the family exhausted and harried. Many of them have nothing left to invest in their marriages or in the nurturing of children.

Fifty-nine percent of boys and girls come home to empty houses every afternoon. . . . This hurried lifestyle also puts great pressure on women. . . . And yet financial pressures and the expectations of others keep them on a treadmill that renders them unable to cope. . . . The two-career family *during the child rearing years* creates a level of stress that is tearing people apart. And it often deprives children of something that they will search for the rest of their lives.[12]

There are many exceptions to the two-career or single-mother pattern, and it is true that stay-at-home mothers can also be harried. But extensive and attentive time with children is clearly essential no matter what the career choices of parents are.

Lacking the time, the energy, or the will to devote ourselves to Christlike parenting, what do we do? We often substitute material largesse, rushing our children to after-school programs and expensive lessons and activities, but we spend too little time sitting quietly as a family talking about things that truly matter. Conversation has power to stimulate minds, strengthen bonds, prevent trouble, and build commitments. Dinnertime is an especially good opportunity for such conversation. But we eat and play together less frequently as parents delegate more responsibility to others—to day cares, baby-sitters, schools, and churches. Let *them* do it.

And television. Television plays a major role in behavior and value formation, and we ignore this at our peril. The average U.S. child watches three to four hours a day, engaging that child for more time than any other daily activity except sleeping. If you do not think the gratuitous sex, violence, humor, language, and coarse behavior shown on television have a formative impact on your children, then the tobacco industry wants you to know that smoking does not cause cancer, the National Rifle Association that guns don't kill people, and advertisers that commercials have no impact on consumers.

Christoph Arnold, elder of a Bruderhof commune in upstate New York, was once asked for an example of a consumer technology that the Bruderhof had tried and abandoned. "VCRs," he replied. "We had VCRs for a while, but then we noticed the children weren't singing. They weren't playing and running and making up songs. They wanted to put in a tape and sit in front of the TV. So we locked up the VCRs. Now the children are singing again."[13]

What do we want our children to be? Who *are* they in the eyes of God—who are they really and truly—they who have been baptized into Christ? For what purpose has God entrusted them to our care? If they are really and truly created by God in God's image and redeemed by God's Son to love and serve him forever, should not our whole purpose as parents and as a family be built around this awesome reality? Should we not do everything possible—in our conversation, our prayers together, our play, our laughter, our daily searching of God's Word, our spending, our sharing with and helping others—to let Christ be the center of our home and our life?

I recently discovered a snapshot of myself, taken when I was eight years old, that immediately became a favorite. It showed a scrawny, unimpressive face behind bent spectacles. Underneath, my father had written in bold letters: "A boy— a man of God." Everyone should have a father like that.

A priest from poverty-stricken Nicaragua observed, "In my country we may ask too much of our young people. But in your country the problem is worse. You ask nothing of the young. You offer them no meaningful vision of life beyond themselves."[14] That is a fearful judgment, when God has something infinitely better and more wonderful for them. Jesus clearly addressed this when he said that "those who want to save their life will lose it, but those who lose their life for me and for the gospel will save it." Then he added, "What good is it for you to gain the whole world, yet forfeit your soul?" (Mark 8:35–36).

The bottom line is clear. We who are parents have been given an awesome privilege—that of nurturing children for the Lord. We walk on holy ground.

## Sabbath Wisdom

We can learn from our scattered lives that we need to retreat. Not in the sense of moving backward, but moving *away* from—distancing, resting, and gaining perspective. This is known in the Hebrew tradition as Sabbath wisdom.

For the Israelites wandering in the desert, Sabbath was a radical idea. Neither Pharaoh nor any other ruler allowed such a thing. A day off? Every week? A beautiful but crazy notion. In the wilderness, survival meant struggling every day with the elements. Yet God wanted his people to rest. "You shall not make yourself or anyone else a slave to work," the commandment might have said, because God included also the servants, strangers, and even the animals! But there was more to it than that. The Israelites needed time to remember God and to remember who they were as God's people. They were to trust God to provide (the lesson also of the manna) and, in trusting, to know that it was not their work, but God who provides for and sustains their lives. Sabbath celebrates the theology of abundance rather than the myth of scarcity.15 It does so in the context of time for restoration.

Much of the world has benefited from this breathtaking reform. The forty-hour work week is one of its eventual fruits in the industrialized North.[16] But we have found ways to frustrate the intent of this limitation to work. Habitually working (by choice or necessity) far beyond the forty hours is one way. Long commutes, drop-offs and pick-ups for day care, school, and various activities, and a backlog of evening and weekend household responsibilities are other ways. Meetings and social obligations add to the mix. The result is scattered, hectic living.

Sabbath wisdom helps us reconsider life, starting at the very center, with God. It may mean abandoning for a day all activities that send family members in different directions or that create more work. Perhaps it suggests pulling the plug on television. Whatever the details, it should mean a break from the pressure, the confusion, the commercial and social distractions of the rest of the week, and time spent deliberately considering how we are doing with our life in God. Maybe we can use the Sunday sermon as a starting point for family discussion about what we might change in order to follow Christ more faithfully and enjoy life with God more completely.

Genuine Sabbath keeping can change our lives. Because it imitates God, who rested from the work of creation, it prepares us to imitate God in other ways as well, such as caring about people who are oppressed. In this way, keeping the Sabbath is not only a retreat from the busyness that confronts us daily, but, writes Marva Dawn, "it plunges us more deeply into the world and its needs because it carries us more deeply into the heart and purposes of God."[17]

Sabbath wisdom helps us reflect on our use of time throughout the week. Time is one of the most valuable of God's gifts, and most of us—even when we feel harried—waste a lot of it. For example, by age sixty-five, the average American will have spent the equivalent of nine full years watching television—thirteen and a half years of waking time![18] Wiser, more efficient use of our time can add immeasurably to the quality of life. Paradoxically, time given to God helps us redeem rather than lose time.

Sabbath is a sharp departure from the culture of mammon. The very idea may evoke fear of silence or boredom. That fear, in turn, may reflect fear of reflection on life or an inability to capitalize on time in creative ways through music, reading, arts and crafts, conversation, or inventive play. Silence and boredom can help us come to terms with ourselves. A child may learn to develop inner resources and self-understanding that would otherwise languish and discover that life is not served up as endlessly entertaining. Adults might learn those things as well.

The Sabbath was meant for celebration, perhaps of the quiet variety, to help us find more joy and beauty in creation, in simple pleasures such as walking and playing and spending time with family or friends. It comes as a gift from God and should not be turned into a set of burdens. "The Sabbath was made for people, not people for the Sabbath" (Mark 2:27).

Just as worship on Sunday morning should spill its meaning into all the hours of the week, so the Sabbath is intended to help us celebrate our walk with God the entire week. Keeping one day holy helps us give the other days to God as well. It suggests a manner of life in which we can break away briefly from time to time each day to pray, reflect, and submit our activity to God's purpose for us. Rising in the morning, however groggy, and turning the day over to God with praise; having prayers at mealtime and family devotions each day; praying silently throughout the day as needs and occasions arise; commending the day and the night to God upon retiring; stepping away from a job to stretch and breathe fresh air; playing music, exercising, or taking a nap—these are among the ways that Sabbath wisdom can help us develop a balanced life more fully responsive to God.

Give yourself a break.

# FIVE

# The Poverty of Riches

God said to him, "You fool! This very night your life will
be demanded from you. Then who will get what you have
prepared for yourself?"
    This is how it will be with those who store up things
for themselves and are not rich toward God.

LUKE 12:20–21

The material creation is good because God made it so. The
creation account in Genesis 1 asserts five times, at five
stages of creation, "And God saw that it was good." And
when creation was complete, "God saw all that he had
made and it was very good" (Gen. 1:31 NIV). Creation is
depicted in various psalms as shouting, singing, clapping,
and skipping for joy, and breaking out in praise to God (e.g.,
Psalms 65, 96, 98, 114, 148). Christianity has been called
the most materialistic of religions, for not only does it
embrace matter as good, but it proclaims that God entered

61

the world in human flesh, the man Jesus of Nazareth. As if that were not enough (and it was not), he died for us and was raised to life again—a resurrected body—to give us the promise of eternal life in resurrected, but transformed bodies. All quite materialistic, honoring the material matter of this earth.

Consistent with this, God has spread a magnificent table before the world in the form of expanding prosperity. Healthier diets and better medical care, housing, clothing, communication, and transportation are gifts to be received with thanksgiving. Why else would God have given humans responsibility as stewards of the earth's resources? We rightly applaud advances that have dramatically saved and improved lives, and brought even to most poor people at least some advantages that were unthinkable for the rich not more than a century ago. These material gains, thankfully received and rightly used, are a blessing to everyone. Coveted for self, however, such gifts become an object of worship—mammon.

Mammon offers a seemingly unlimited array of attractions, promising that these will make us happy and give life meaning. Instead it provides satisfactions that are fleeting, but addictive. Like drugs, the dose of mammon has to be regularly available and perhaps periodically increased in order to keep our satisfaction at an acceptable level.

Mammon also makes us anxious. Whether about food or stock portfolio, we begin to worry. In both Matthew and Luke, concern about money is directly linked by Jesus to anxiety.[1] His words are placed in the context of addressing his disciples and the crowds that came to hear him. The crowds were composed mainly of common people, most of them poor. So the problem is *preoccupation* with mammon more than the *amount* of mammon. Poor people are apt to worry about food and clothing, rich people to covet much more. Either way, trust is the first casualty—a terrible loss, because trust is exactly what God wants from us and what lies at the heart of our relationship with God.

If trust is the first casualty, love is the next. Addiction to mammon makes us forget others. Preoccupied with keeping what we have or getting what we do not have, the needs of others fade from our thoughts. It is not so much that we wish them harm as that we have no wishes for them at all. They become nonentities, abstractions. Writer James Fallows observes:

> The way a rich nation thinks about its poor will always be convoluted. The richer people become in general, the easier it theoretically becomes for them to share with people who are left out. But the richer people become, the less they naturally stay in touch with realities of life on the bottom, and the more they naturally prefer to be excited about their own prospects rather than concerned about someone else's.[2]

"I know how very hard it is to be rich and still keep the milk of human kindness," the late archbishop Dom Helder Camara of Recife, Brazil, said.[3]

The poor are not the only ones who suffer. The rich fool who stored up things withheld them from others, but he also prevented himself from becoming rich toward God (Luke 12:16–21). Those who bought and sold slaves were themselves warped and twisted by treating people as possessions. The same is true for us in a more subtle way if we hang on to our possessions rather than sharing them with people in need. When mammon is cherished, people—affluent as well as poor—are dehumanized, for to love things reduces people to commodity status.

Because the pursuit and accumulation of wealth does not and cannot give transcendent meaning to life, it fails the test of eternity. It can pamper our bodies and stroke our egos for a while, but the "while" inevitably comes to an end. Death soon takes our loved ones and our loved things from us. So the rich man in the parable who said to himself, "Take life easy; eat, drink and be merry," was a fool for having fastened his hope on prosperity when that very night he faced death (Luke 12:19–21). He forgot that he brought nothing into the world and could take nothing out.

For all of these reasons, kneeling at the altar of mammon impoverishes us, for to be "rich in things, but poor in soul"[4] is to be very poor indeed.

## Having or Being?

We are human *beings*, not human *havings*. God loves us for who we are, not what we have. To love mammon is to confuse having with being. We see this reflected in children for whom the toys they get or the brand of sneakers or jeans they wear become badges of status. Peers who wear the wrong kind are readily humiliated by the others. Both the haves and the have-nots, however, accept "having" as a standard.

When we see this in children, we recognize how unfair is the judgment, how insecure are those who make it, and how pathetic is the status to which they aspire. But are these children not mirror images of us? In our culture, labels and style of clothes make a difference to people. The size and location of a house, the kind of car, one's position and one's salary (or allowance) become status symbols. You are what you have.

That sends a chilling message to people who don't have much. But it also entangles people of wealth with a false sense of worth. No matter how much you have, there is always more to be gotten. Measured against those who have more, your life doesn't seem so full after all.

To confuse having with being is to worship the gift rather than the giver, fragments of creation instead of the Creator. It is also to forget that God alone determines our worth, not what we have or what others think of us. God has made us in his own image, to be like him in our creativity and work, but most of all in love and generosity. Though in our fallen state we don't do that very well, God has rescued us in Jesus Christ. Through the cross, God has declared us righteous in his eyes by virtue of forgiveness. Through Christ, we are sons and daughters of the Most High. And we would exchange that status to be measured by a pair of sneakers?

I exaggerate, of course. Most of us do not value ourselves wholly by our possessions. But who can deny that the culture of mammon has had a huge impact on how all of us regard ourselves?

Let me tell you about Bryce and Ellen, a couple in their mid-thirties. They have two sons and a daughter, and on Sundays the family attends church more often than not. Bryce manages about twenty people in a medium-sized accounting firm. He receives a good salary and is on a path that he believes may eventually move him into a circle of company executives, so he goes to work early, often stays late, and usually works some on weekends. Ellen has a part-time job with a public relations firm, which allows her to manage the kids and take care of the house. None of this is easy, but it has enabled them to buy a house in an upscale neighborhood and a lot of recreational hardware, including a raft of toys, a couple of TVs for the children's rooms, and a small yacht.

Bryce and Ellen already talk about one day taking early retirement and moving to a place where they can enjoy year-round outdoor sports. Though deeply in debt, they are able to make timely payments and take pride in contributing "more than most" to church in dollar amount, which at 2.5 percent of their income is about average for church members. They would be astonished—probably offended—to have anyone suggest that they are beholden to mammon. Yet their plans and dreams, and the dreams they are nourishing in their children, are overwhelmingly directed that way.

Jesus was no killjoy. "I have come that they may have life, and have it to the full" (John 10:10)—"have it more abundantly" reads the better known King James Version. The life

Jesus came to give was one of undeserved and unrestrained love, a life of peace and joy in the Holy Spirit. He came to invite us into the Father's kingdom. That is the abundant life. But it is measured by *being* rather than *having*. Compared to the life Jesus offers, mammon in any amount is poverty.

In calling us to deny ourselves, take up the cross, and follow him, Jesus is offering us rewards of *being* that are stunningly better than the *having* we are asked to give up—in this life *and* in the age to come (Luke 18:29–30). "It would seem," C. S. Lewis wrote, "that Our Lord finds our desires not too strong, but too weak. We are half-hearted creatures, fooling about with drink and sex and ambition when infinite joy is offered us, like an ignorant child who wants to go on making mud pies in a slum because he cannot image what is meant by the offer of a holiday at the sea. We are far too easily pleased."[5]

## Mammon as Master

Sin does not come from material things but, as Jesus said, from the heart (Matt. 15:19). Sins of the heart—pride, lust, greed, envy, covetousness—lead people to obtain, value, and use possessions wrongly. The biblical case against mammon is not against possessions as such, but against possessions gaining control of us. It is our attachment, our submission to them, that is idolatrous.

Just as possessions do not condemn us, the lack of them or even the surrender of them does not save us, either. The apostle Paul wrote, "If I give all I possess to the poor . . . but do not have love, I gain nothing" (1 Cor. 13:3). Without love, responding to Jesus by selling all that you have and giving it to the poor doesn't count. The love that Paul says is essential, however, is not romantic love or simple friendship, but a compassion that embraces the undeserving, a compassion that finds its origin in God's compassion for us

66

as revealed in the life and death of Jesus. Without that undeserved gift of love from God, our most sacrificial actions are futile attempts to become righteous on terms that allow us to get the credit. "Pray for me that I not loosen my grip on the hands of Jesus even under the guise of ministering to the poor," said Mother Teresa.[6]

Possessions readily take over. "The most natural expansion of the self is the expansion through possessions," Reinhold Niebuhr wrote.[7] We become enamored of them, infatuated as a lover might become infatuated, and give our hearts to them. Instead of possessing things, things begin to possess us. As consumers, we are the subjects and the things we consume are the objects. Or so we imagine. But what if, by consuming or wanting to consume things, we become infected with a desire that consumes us?

In D. H. Lawrence's story, "The Rocking Horse Winner," the family of a little boy, Paul, lives way beyond its means. They are always desperate to get more money. By chance, Paul discovers that if he races his rocking horse, the names of winning race horses mysteriously come to him. The family cashes in. But getting the winning names requires increasingly faster rocking and Paul finally dies of exhaustion in his attempt to satisfy the appetite of the household for more money.[8]

In *Whatever Became of Sin?* psychiatrist Karl Menninger wrote of wealthy patients driven to mental illness from greed. One, having attempted suicide, brightened at the suggestion of giving to charity as a memorial to his father— but did nothing. "He existed for a few more years, then died, prematurely, to the satisfaction of his heirs and business associates who were not yet in his predicament, although they suffered from the same 'disease.'"[9]

The poor as well as the rich are susceptible to the lure of mammon. Poor people may covet possessions and envy the rich. More commonly, worry grinds them down. As Thomas Cahill has noted, Jesus was "far gentler in dealing with the stumbling block of worry," than with the arrogance and greed of the privileged.[10] Even so, Jesus saw that worries, as well as the riches and pleasures of life, could choke out the Word of God and pull people away from the kingdom (Luke 8:14).

Both worry and greed are forms of looking to possessions for security. "When we seek for security in possessions we are trying to drive out care with care," Dietrich Bonhoeffer wrote, "and the net result is the precise opposite of our anticipations. The fetters which bind us to our possessions prove to be cares themselves."[11]

Security in possessions represents a hedge for survival, and so it reflects the fear of death. That should not surprise us. If this life is the only life in which we hope, it is the only one worth investing in; and there is a certain desperation in doing so. But Jesus calls us to enter the kingdom!

Churches are not exempt from the mastery of mammon. "The contemporary American church is so largely enculturated in the American ethos of consumerism that it has little power to believe or to act," writes Walter Brueggemann in *The Prophetic Imagination*.[12] Some churches have prospered by offering a gospel of prosperity detached from the cross, in this way stroking the greed of congregants. More frequently, pastors cushion the truth of Jesus to affluent congregations, either because the pastors themselves are numbed by the culture or because they fear offending members and putting their own jobs in harm's way. Either path can make the church a chaplaincy for the culture of affluence.

"You cannot serve God and mammon," Jesus said (Matt. 6:24 RSV). He seemed to be addressing people who wanted to have it both ways. "Jesus does not excoriate the tax collectors, since as a group it seems they did not live in a both/and way of life," writes John Haughey. "They were up front with their fraud and extortion. But he was not so gentle with the religious leadership who tried and in many cases succeeded in having the best of both the world of material security and religion. . . . [T]heir lives were a lesson in trying to have God, material security and honor all at the same time."[13] That was a persistent temptation for them and for Israelites before them, and it is a temptation for us as well. Most of us, says Haughey, are working both sides of the street, but Jesus allows only one master. We *cannot* serve God and mammon. God passionately wants our hearts and knows that our hearts and our treasure follow the same path.

## Mammon as Servant

When mammon is master, a host of evils follow. We are diminished in spirit and others are neglected. Time, talents, and treasures get disproportionately given to self-enhancing pursuits. A world of plenty for everyone becomes a place of greed, starvation, division, and conflict. The headlines change day by day, but the story stays the same.

God, however, is on a mission to win our hearts and set us free from mammon. Mammon can then be put to good use. That is exceedingly good news, because mammon makes a terrible master but a magnificent servant. A servant, of course, cannot be in charge, for he does not own or control anything. His only legitimate role is to carry out the intentions of the master. So mammon—that pretender, that pseudo-god— must be put in its proper place and made obedient to God. This is not the language of compromise, but of transformation. The biblical words for it are *repentance* and *faith*.[14]

What does it mean to place mammon in service to God? It means that everything we have and everything we earn must be seen in an entirely different light. The critical question is no longer "What do I want?" or "What can we afford to do?" but "How can we use what God has given us to carry out God's will?" For this question the Bible gives us no pat formulas, but it does send some clear signals.

Jesus emphatically and repeatedly connected use of money with generosity to the poor, just as throughout his entire ministry he reached out to poor and marginalized people. Consider his description of the final judgment:

> Then the King will say to those on his right, "Come, you who are blessed by my Father; take your inheritance, the kingdom prepared for you since the creation of the world. For I was hungry and you gave me something to eat, I was thirsty and you gave me something to drink, I was a stranger and you invited me in, I needed clothes and you clothed me, I was sick and you looked after me, I was in prison and you came to visit me."
>
> **MATTHEW 25:34–36**

In saying this, Jesus was faithful to the Hebrew Scriptures, in particular the prophets, who proclaimed justice for the oppressed; however, he went beyond the prophets by identifying *himself* with the oppressed and with those who help them.

Identification with the oppressed is clearly essential. For this to happen, personal contact and, if possible, personal friendship with those who suffer is an invaluable step. This can be done, for example, by connecting with a family struggling in the absence of an imprisoned father, helping in a soup kitchen, visiting the lonely, sick, or aged, assisting the physically or mentally impaired, becoming a special friend to a neglected child, or helping your church to become engaged with people such as these. In doing so, you discover the humbling joy of receiving much more than you give.

"The shell of isolation must be shattered before compassion can begin to grow," writes Don McClanen,[15] who has specialized in getting people of means on "reverse mission" visits to developing countries. Pamela Stephenson was one such missioner who visited Shishu Bhavan, a home started by Mother Teresa in Calcutta for abandoned children. Stephenson's life was changed by a four-year-old boy. "I still can't talk about him, because I just cry," she said. So she wrote a poem:

> Always a barrier,
> Preventing me from loving.
>   Little boy standing by my side,
> Beautiful hair, hideous sores on his legs,
> Open wounds, I don't want to pick him up,
> Yet his arms reach up to me, asking to come.
> I let him struggle, hoping he would go away.
>   But he persisted, until I could no longer refuse.
>   Reluctantly from behind, I pulled him to my lap.
>   Only then
>           I saw that he was blind.
> My heart went out to him, my shell was cracked
> As he clung desperately to me.
> Close as we were it was not close enough.
> I held him tightly and resting my head on his,
> Wept in despair.
>             Blind in Calcutta—what hope for him
> With me so blind?
>           Observed in him, the child in me
> And wept again
> With joy and pain
>   Experiencing the mystery of a Love that overcomes.[16]

How much Pamela Stephenson gave to the child is not clear. That the child gave much to Pamela Stephenson is abundantly clear. Even in such brief encounters are lives and hopes fashioned.

## Servant Churches

One of the most striking examples of mammon as servant was the offering among the Gentile churches for the relief of Jewish Christians in Judea. The early church there, composed mainly of those poor and socially despised people that Jesus was determined to include, suffered extreme hardship because of a famine that afflicted all of Palestine in the middle of the first century A.D. One can hardly read Paul's account of the generosity of the churches of Macedonia (2 Cor. 8), without being deeply moved by the love of those Gentile believers for Christian Jews far away whom they did not know. Many Jewish Christians felt alienated from Gentile Christians, and Paul was eager to help break that barrier with the gift of love. Paul writes of these Macedonians that, despite their own poverty, they *begged* for the privilege of contributing (v. 4). With joy and generosity, they gave "beyond their ability" (v. 3). But, Paul said, they gave themselves first to the Lord (v. 5). Using their example, Paul reminds the Christians in Corinth of "the grace of our Lord Jesus Christ, that though he was rich, yet for your sake he became poor, so that you through his poverty might become rich" (v. 9).

Paul, too, stands out as an example, for this offering of reconciliation and love mattered more to him than his life. Consider his stirring moments with the elders of the church at Ephesus while on the way to Jerusalem (Acts 20:18–38). Paul believed that prison and hardship awaited him there—which it did. But he was determined to press on, and before he left he spoke these words of encouragement: "In everything I did, I showed you that by this kind of hard work we must help the weak, remembering the words the Lord Jesus himself said: 'It is more blessed to give than to receive'" (v. 35).

Churches today occasionally stand out as models of putting mammon in service to Christ. St. Pius X Catholic Church in Indianapolis established sister-church relations with St. Philip Neri, a local inner-city church, and also with a church in El Salvador. Besides joint activities with St. Philip Neri, once or twice a year St. Pius has a group of ten to twelve members, sometimes their youth teams, visit El Salvador. The church is contributing 22 percent of its offerings to outreach, which includes support for the sister churches. A big factor in generating parish involvement was a four-month sabbatical by St. Pius's pastor, Martin Peter, with Catholic Relief Services and Maryknoll missionaries in Africa.

Grace Lutheran Church in Des Moines, Washington, decided in the late 1970s to postpone the building of a new sanctuary and instead raise a million dollars for world hunger. The congregation has raised $1.6 million for hunger relief since then, and puts 30 percent of its offerings toward benevolence, which includes sister churches in Haiti and Jamaica, youth groups visiting Mexico and doing mission work in the States, and its own shelter for the homeless in the winter. Once again the pastor, Ed Marquart, provided catalytic leadership.

Eastminster Presbyterian Church in Wichita, Kansas, had designed a new sanctuary when a devastating earthquake struck Guatemala, destroying homes and churches. One lay person posed a simple question: "How can we set out to buy an ecclesiastical Cadillac when our brothers and sisters in Guatemala have just lost their little Volkswagen?" So they settled for a smaller building program and borrowed money to rebuild twenty-six Guatemalan churches and twenty-eight pastors' homes.[17] Soon they pledged more money for an evangelical seminary there. These efforts jump-started a more intentional mission outreach program, which focuses especially on frontier missions. This ministry includes Bible translation, literacy work among Muslim women, work among the "untouchables" in India, and trips all over the world by various work teams and medical teams from the congregation. Eastminster allocates more than a million dollars a year—one-third to one-half of its income—to missions, reports Tom Edwards, its current pastor.

Those are models. Responding to them can start with prayer and conversation at home and at church. At home, perhaps it means teaching your children to see money in a different way and helping them discern what to spend and what to share. Perhaps it means moving to a smaller house or keeping that old car a while longer in order to contribute more to the poor and to the mission of your church. Maybe it means investing in funds that are socially and environmentally beneficial. Perhaps it means reexamining your life insurance beneficiaries, rewriting your will, or planning a trust in order to leave part of your estate to an organization such as Bread for the World, Habitat for Humanity, or your church's overseas ministry. If you own a business, maybe it means taking steps to share its blessings more equitably with your employees.

For some, it might mean actually selling possessions and giving to the poor. More often it suggests a variation of that principle: contributing generously, as resources permit—not just chipping in a few dollars we don't need. I think of David and Robin Miner, parents of two children in college, who share much of their talent and money to help hungry people. Robin puts it this way: "God calls me to be loving and generous. I pray about this and work when I'd rather not, in part because it is the path by which I can be the most generous. I give because it is a way to love."

Whatever the details, it starts with becoming captive to the grace of our Lord Jesus Christ and deciding to put mammon in service to God. The obstacle for me is not that I don't understand this. The obstacle is trusting God enough to do it.

## The Riches of Gratitude

When things are valued too much, they lose their value because they nourish a never-satisfied craving for more. Conversely, when things are received as gifts from God and used obediently in service to God, they are enriched with gratitude. As sages have said, contentment lies not in obtaining things you want, but in giving thanks for what you have. Of the two ways to become rich, gratitude is far better.

Some years ago, while visiting Mozambique during a time of war and famine, a few of us traveling for World Vision came upon a small encampment of refugees who had fled their village in search of food. Many villagers had already died. The several dozen survivors were living in makeshift tents, foraging for berries and nuts and creatures that supplemented their meager ration of daily grain from CARE. They had nothing but the tattered clothes they wore and a few pots for cooking. But they were alive. We spent some time listening to gut-wrenching personal experiences. As we got ready to leave, some of the women began dancing in a circle, singing and clapping, their faces beaming as they moved first in one direction, then the other. They repeated the same words over and over. I finally asked someone, "What are they singing?" The man translated, "We have food. We have clothes. We have everything!" These people, destitute beyond belief, were rich in gratitude.

Gratitude is not one of my strong points. Perhaps for that reason, I cherish the conviction that in heaven God will give us the gift of completely thankful hearts. I have no idea what the furniture or living quarters or technology will look like. I am confident, however, that our hearts will be filled with a gratitude so deep that it will give us unrestrained and never-ending joy.

In the Old Testament, prosperity is regarded by the faithful as a gift. To regard it as such is to avoid the deceits of pride and greed and to honor God with its use. Adversity may be a judgment, but it can also be a gift. The apostle Paul faced his share of suffering, but he found it grounds for thanks because of the character and hope that it built (Rom. 5:1–5). Imprisoned in Rome, Paul wrote to believers in Philippi a letter of thanksgiving and joy in which he expressed the conviction that God was using his imprisonment to advance the gospel (Phil. 1:12–30). And he tells the Philippians that he has learned to be content whether well fed or hungry, in abundance or in want. He gave thanks for all of it (4:12–13).

The Gospel of Luke records the healing of ten lepers (17:11–19). On their way to show themselves to the priests (who could vouch for their health, so they could return to society), only one came back to thank Jesus, and he was a foreigner. What is most remarkable to me in this account is that after asking, "Where are the other nine?" Jesus told the man, "Your faith has made you well" (v. 19). Really? But *ten* were made well, though nine of them showed no evidence of faith. How then can Jesus say to this one (a foreigner, at that), "Your faith has made you well"? Is the clue that "has made you well" can be translated "has saved you, rescued you, made you whole"? Jesus seems to have told the man in effect, "The other nine may no longer have leprosy, but *you* have been made whole—physically and spiritually healed—because you have faith, faith that you have shown by your gratitude."

The other nine had been healed. This man was whole.

# SIX

# The Sorrow of Pleasure

Even in laughter the heart may ache,
and joy may end in grief.

**—PROVERBS 14:13** NIV

The pleasure and happiness of people must be one of God's delights. After all, creation includes endless sights and sounds of immense beauty as well as friendship and intimacy, laughter and play, satisfaction in accomplishing things, and much, much more. Pleasure was surely intended to be part of our enjoyment of life with God.

People do many things for pleasure. They watch sunsets, tell jokes, visit friends, play games, sports, and music, drive cars, and go shopping. Walk through a mall or flip on the television and you are soon flooded with pain-avoiding and pleasure-promising images. They come to us in so many different forms that choosing pleasure is like selecting food in a supermarket with plenty of things to suit everyone's taste.

Pleasure comes from God. But it becomes a problem when, as is our disposition, we begin to place trust in it. People often seek pleasure hoping it will bring them happiness, the pursuit of which is embodied in the Declaration of Independence. There, along with life and liberty, it is given the status of an inalienable right—an indication of the importance we attach both to freedom and to the pursuit of happiness. As our culture has grown more affluent, pleasure has become an increasingly sought after commodity. Observers routinely conclude that Western civilization, and the United States in particular, is hedonistic: deeply committed to pleasure. The pursuit of pleasure has become a major characteristic of affluent cultures.

Like mammon, pleasure thrives on rising expectations. If others have (or seem to have) more than we do, we may feel cheated. In a pleasure-escalating society, temptations tend to expand when others increasingly enjoy what we do not.

Pleasure can seduce. In the movie *Monty Python and the Holy Grail,* one of the knights is captured by witches. Instead of being tortured, he faces beautiful women who tempt him. Just as he is about to succumb, his fellow knights break into the castle for the rescue—only to discover that the knight doesn't want to be rescued, at least not yet.[1]

Sometimes pleasure tantalizes us to do things that are morally objectionable. More often, however, it spreads before us attractions that are perfectly acceptable but can make life a self-indulgent enterprise. Pleasure, like mammon, can turn our hearts away from God and from the needs of others, and prompt us to center life on ourselves. When that happens, we may have no desire to be rescued.

Pleasure, in that case, carries the seeds of sorrow. Pleasure valued as a gift from God contains elements of joy. Pleasure detached from God and idolized, however, invests itself in sorrow. Like mammon, it seems to promise what will fill our lives with satisfaction, then disappoints us because it cannot do so. It gives us no transcendent meaning and becomes another god that fails. As a way of life, pleasure offers an ethic of "eat, drink, and be merry for tomorrow we die." Therein lies its sorrow, for the bottom line is death. It is the sorrow of lonely New Year's Eve revelers, the sorrow of an alcohol or drug abuser, the sorrow of a sexual affair, the expressionless face emerging from a pornographic movie, the headlines on a supermarket tabloid. Like a final bash for supporters of a failed political candidate, it is the sorrow of living for the moment, knowing that beyond the moment everything is lost. In short, it is pleasure shorn of hope.

Reflecting on her early experience with a literary set in New York, Dorothy Day, founder of the Catholic Worker movement, spoke of "the sorrow of hedonism." Her contemporary, Edna St. Vincent Millay, the first woman to win the Pulitzer Prize for poetry, personified that sorrow. Frail of health, she was promiscuous with men and women, drank, partied, used drugs, had affairs and abortions, married, had more affairs, and died an alcoholic at age fifty-eight. "I have been ecstatic; but I have not been happy," she wrote early in her career.[2] As a high school student, I knew nothing of her life, but was struck by the melancholy brilliance of one of her poems:

> My candle burns at both ends;
> It will not last the night;
> But ah, my foes, and oh, my friends—
> It gives a lovely light!

The poem is clearly autobiographical, but I think she had it backwards. It is not the lovely light that has the last word, but the fact that it will not last the night. That lovely light, like all trusted pleasure, is laden with sorrow.

## Pleasure as Master

If pleasure idolized contains the seeds of sadness, we may be investing in sadness for our children without realizing it. Not a happy thought. We may shower them with toys, games, TVs, videos, sports equipment, trips, and entertainment of all kinds. The appetite for these is insatiable, and unless by example and instruction we carefully set limits and relate those limits to life's purpose, we are training our children to turn their lives over to a soul-imperiling idolatry.

The problem is not that pleasure is bad. In the first chapter of Genesis, God pronounces creation "good." The Hebrew word connotes beautiful as well as good. It pleases God to let us enjoy creation. It is not pleasure that condemns us, nor the lack of it that saves us. The problem emerges because pleasure, like mammon, can capture our hearts and become an end in itself. All of us, rich and poor, are vulnerable to this captivity, especially in the most tender years of life. Pleasure then becomes master and replaces our affection for God and our compassion for others.

Pleasure has become master of much of our Western culture partly because of the dramatic increase in wealth during the last half-century, and partly because society has largely adopted naturalism (the belief that everything has a material origin and does not come from intelligent design) as an operating philosophy. Naturalism often exists side by side with expressed faith in God, but it is clearly naturalism and not God that dominates our culture and informs our thoughts and habits. As a result we tend to be "practical atheists"—people who speak of God but act largely without reference to God. In that case, to pursue pleasure as one's aim in life is perfectly natural, and immediate gratification comes to be expected. This has led to a society in which people seek their own fulfillment with little regard for the common good.

In this context, we should not be surprised at the coarsening of entertainment, the flaunting of gratuitous sex at the very young, the increasing use of obscenities, and the continuing flood of violence. In this way, pleasure attracts money and money pushes pleasure to new limits of acceptability in a downward spiral. The only question seems to be, "What sells?" and the motto for the public, "If it feels good, do it." This is pleasure as master.

Pleasure as master has had a particularly destructive impact on sexual mores and families. Premature stimulation of the young, coupled with a permissive attitude toward casual sex, has led to predictable consequences. Invest in illicit sex and one can expect the dividends of loneliness and scarred lives. Intimacy without commitment is hardly preparation for enduring marriages and stable families. This kind of pleasure is not what you would call a victimless sin, for the victims are strewn everywhere, most of them casualties of neglect on the part of affluent sinners who were too busy serving themselves to notice.

A great illusion is abroad in the land (whispered, I am told, by some serpent) that God is a wet blanket and that if we follow God, we will be cheated of the pleasure we are entitled to, robbed of fulfillment and happiness. A companion illusion is that if we do what we feel like doing, we will be blessed.

The drink is intoxicating. But it is pure poison.

## Points of Pleasure

There are certain key aspects of pleasure that produce turning points in life. One of these has to do with instant gratification, a problem that has grown with affluence and media influence. A reason for alarm is how early the expectation of instant gratification takes hold, moving us far beyond genuine needs. The marshmallow test illustrates this. A researcher tells a four-year-old child, "I am leaving for a few minutes to run an errand and you can have this marshmallow while I am gone, but if you wait until I return, you can have *two* marshmallows." Several decades ago, Stanford University researchers ran that test and then a dozen years later studied the same children. They found that those who had grabbed the single marshmallow tended to be more troubled in adolescence and scored an average of 210 points less on standard achievement tests.[3] Character training begins much earlier and with greater consequences than most parents realize. Pleasure can harm the very young, precisely when we think we are helping them by giving them what they want.

Another pleasure-related turning point is the triumph of romantic love as an ideal. Unfortunately, the search for romance does not prepare people well for marriage and family life. Dating and courtship as currently practiced—quite a new phenomenon in human history—tend to focus on physical attraction and superficial interests. More attention is often given to preparation for the wedding than to preparation for the marriage. In all of this, the pursuit of pleasure takes precedence over the pursuit of purpose. The idea of love as commitment and marriage as the bonding of husband and wife around a higher goal are shortchanged; yet it is within this context that romance and affection have the best chance of flourishing. For Christians, that higher goal is clear, but unless young people are trained long before adolescence to begin all things with Christ and to think about courtship and marriage in terms of his design for our lives, shipwreck may lurk in the shadows.

That leads to the next pleasure-related turning point: troubled marriages. All marriages encounter difficulties. If approached within the framework of a mutual desire to follow Christ, difficulties can usually be surmounted, and in the process, the bonds of affection and loyalty between partners and with God can be strengthened. But if self-fulfillment is uppermost (and abuse and domination are among the forms it takes), divorce is a frequent outcome. A failed marriage any time is cause for remorse, even when unavoidable; but when children are involved, it is especially regrettable because it shatters a vital part of their childhood and most of the time leaves deep, and sometimes debilitating, scars. What may be parental choice in favor of self-fulfillment looks more like a nightmare to children, who are casualties of freedom *from* rather than freedom *for* commitment.

Consider children an additional turning point. There are great pleasures in marrying and having children; but in some ways, childrearing and marriage involve the opposite of pleasure, for they require unrelenting attention and bring many frustrations. These, too, are gifts of God because they compel us to grow into responsible adults. If children, like marriage, are sought for pleasure, they are likely to disappoint us, and may even become sources of displeasure that threaten the marriage. Children are a long-term investment of the highest sort, and we need to build that investment steadily with painstaking faith, love, and prayer. Then the pleasures and satisfaction can be great.

These turning points have common ground in our growing disposition to put short-term pleasure ahead of lasting satisfaction. When Esau, famished, sold his birthright to Jacob for a bowl of stew, he despised his heritage for momentary advantage. Esau became a metaphor of the temptation to live for this world at the cost of eternal life. So it is with us if we let pleasure become master.

## Pleasure as Gift

Philip Yancey has written, "Evil's greatest triumph may be its success in portraying religion as an enemy of pleasure when, in fact, religion accounts for pleasure's source."[4] Yancey observes that he has never seen a book on "the problem of pleasure." Since Christians are challenged to explain the origin of human suffering in the presence of a good and loving God, shouldn't atheists be required to explain the origin of something as wonderful as pleasure in the alleged absence of such a God?

That God created everything good is no mere abstraction. God has a heart of love for his creatures and delights in their delight. It is not the case that God is a grumpy old codger who gets annoyed when one of us feels good. Pleasure and happiness are gifts from a God so generous that he makes his sun shine on good and bad people alike, and sends rain on the just and on the unjust. God created the gift of sight and spread creation before us in magnificent technicolor. God created the gift of hearing and the beauty of music along with a thousand other sounds, the taste of wine, the touch of an infant, the hug of a child, the intimacy of sex, the warmth of memories, the laughter of friends. We savor these the more by knowing the giver and receiving them with thanksgiving.

Pleasure and happiness are by-products. Make either your goal and you spoil or lose it. "You can't get second things by putting them first," said C. S. Lewis; "you can get second things only by putting first things first."[5] People who worship health are not healthy. And when we make pleasure more than a servant, it soon ceases to please.

There once were two dogs. The first dog spent all of the time and energy it could muster chasing its tail. The second dog watched and finally asked, "Why do you chase your tail all the time?" The first dog replied, "I have studied these matters, and I have learned that happiness lies in my tail. That is why I chase it." "I understand," said the second dog, "for I, too, have studied and learned that happiness lies in my tail. But I have also learned that if I chase my tail I never catch it; but if I go about my business, my tail always follows." Pursue happiness and it eludes us. Go about life's intended purpose, and a measure of happiness follows.

As society becomes more affluent, happiness increasingly appears as something we have a right to pursue, as an entitlement. We feel cheated, perhaps even angry at God, if it doesn't come. If happiness is our aim in life, we are apt to make religion a means to self-fulfillment, which is why feel-good spirituality has become extremely popular. But faith that has as its goal the gratifying of our own sense of well-being turns worship inward upon ourselves rather than upward in praise and thanksgiving, and outward in service.

To be sure, faith in Christ does bring deep personal sat-isfaction. Faith lifts us up through our identity as children of God. This happens, however, not when we affirm our-selves, but when we come to God as empty-handed sinners to receive the grace of forgiveness—God's great affirmation of us. Obedience follows. God offers us a crown, but always by way of the cross. The path is not one of gratifying our-selves, but following Christ and serving others.

Everything flows from that, including the gift of pleasure.

## Joy

Jesus promised joy, not happiness. He called those who enter the kingdom "blessed," a word that connotes a peace and wholeness much deeper than merely "happy." Not that he is against happiness, but he wishes to give us a much greater reward. No transitory experience, joy is an endur-ing gift that comes to us through the work of Christ and the presence of Christ within us, even—and sometimes espe-cially—in the face of suffering.

Joy may be experienced on rare occasions as ecstasy; but ecstasy does not produce joy, for without joy, ecstasy leaves us empty in its wake. More often joy is received as a quiet but profound satisfaction, grounded in the peace of God. To begin living eternally in the presence of pure compas-sion is to be blessed with a profound joy.

Joy is Dorothy Day, who after an unanchored life in the company of emerging literary figures, bore out of wedlock a daughter whose birth stirred a happiness within her that prompted a full return to faith. She had her daughter baptized, rejoined the church, and founded the Catholic Worker, a movement whose hospitality for destitute people and work for justice and nonviolence has touched the conscience of the church and the nation.

Joy is St. Francis, who gave up wealth and pleasure to become an impoverished fool for Christ, embracing lepers and offering himself so completely to a life of poverty and preaching to the poor that he became a major force for renewal in a moribund Western Christendom.

Joy is Corrie ten Boom, a young Dutch Christian who risked her life again and again to rescue Jews from the Holocaust during World War II, and while in a concentration camp, praised God for the lice and bedbugs that kept the Nazi guards at bay.

Joy is Ed Mullins, who drives a shuttle bus for car renters at the St. Louis airport and treats them like cherished friends, because he sees the job as part of his Christian calling.

Joy is Maria Nuri of Guatemala City, who gave up a profitable profession of telling fortunes and casting spells, even though it meant moving with her son to a shack at the edge of a ravine. "I don't feel that I gave up anything," she said. "I now know Jesus as my Lord and the Savior of my life, and nothing can take that away from me."[6]

These people found a treasure of unsurpassed value. That treasure is Jesus Christ, "who for the joy set before him endured the cross" (Heb. 12:2). So we arrive at the strange paradox that the way of the cross is the way to joy.

We may infer that the degree of joy experienced is related to the degree of love perceived and returned.

Joy, however, is never a product of our making. It is a gift of God, a fruit of the Holy Spirit, bracketed by Paul between love and peace (Gal. 5:22). To be invited into the presence of God and to live in God's presence while we are being formed each day by Christ—this is joy. And as if that were not enough, God has given each of us a unique assignment here on earth. What honor or privilege could possibly compare?

"Ask and you will receive, and your joy will be complete," Jesus said (John 16:24). But the asking, he said, is to be "in my name." That rules out asking for what *we* want, with God at our beck and call, and points rather to seeking what *God* wants for us and for others in Christ. The first kind of prayer would make God our servant; in the second, we become servants of God. "Thy will be done." When that becomes the longing of our hearts for which we pray, our prayers are answered without fail—though not always without pain—and joy follows.

# SEVEN

# The Weakness of Power

This was the secret of his personality:
he loved people more than power.

**—Yves Congar of John XXIII[1]**

People have power. In varying degrees, through mental or physical prowess, personality or position, they have the ability to shape the way they and others live.

Power is a gift of God intended to be used in love for the care of the earth and its creatures, especially the human family. So used, power is a blessing. Used for other purposes, power does great harm. The care of the earth, for example, can become abuse of the earth.

Power is seductive and, like pleasure, it is closely related to mammon. All three have a magnetic appeal that can pull us away from loving God and others. It is no accident, then, that as monastic life and various religious communities emerged within the church, their members took vows of poverty, chastity, and obedience—choosing poverty over mammon, chastity rather than pleasure, and obedience instead of power.

The desire for power is reflected in the Genesis account of the fall, when the serpent told Eve that if she and Adam would eat the forbidden fruit, "your eyes will be opened, and *you will be like God*, knowing everything" (Gen. 3:5 NIV, emphasis added).[2] An awesome prospect! The irony was that they had been created in the image of God. Their grab for power corrupted rather than enhanced that likeness.

The temptation of Jesus was the mirror opposite of the fall. It reports a struggle for the heart of Jesus, an attempt to get Jesus to use the power he had for personal advantage. The temptation belongs in the context of what the Gospels show to be an overwhelming desire on the part of the people for a messiah who would liberate them from oppressive Roman rule. So when Satan showed Jesus the kingdoms of the world in all their splendor, it was as though he said (repeatedly in Jesus' ministry, the Gospel of Luke suggests), "Look, here's the world as it really is, governed by the powerful and given to me. I'm the one who controls it, for as you can plainly see, might makes right on this earth. And you can have it all—not merely a piece of it, but all of it. Just give me your allegiance and you will be my son. The power and the glory of the world will be *yours*." This was, in more common prose, the call to fulfill the dreams of the people and become their earthly liberator.

Centuries earlier, the lust for power and its consequences were evident in the rise of the kingship in Israel, which prompted a stern warning against the king, who would multiply horses, wives, silver, and gold (Deut. 17:14–17). These signified power, pleasure, and riches, as well as pride because they were symbols of high status. They also showed how tightly interwoven mammon is with power and pleasure.

Even David, the model of a *good* king, accumulated wealth and added wives. Infatuation for Bathsheba eventually led David to have her husband Uriah killed.

The introduction of kings in Israel launched a social, as well as a political, revolution. As the kings centralized power, wealth also became increasingly concentrated in the hands of a privileged minority. Those with ambition and ability often developed profitable connections to royalty, while some of the least fortunate were pressed into forced labor. The well-to-do bought land from indebted families, so large estates began replacing small farms. Distinct classes emerged. The gap between rich and poor widened, abetted by cheating and bribery, prompting prophets to denounce this injustice as a sin against God and the people.

People today reflect the same impulse toward abuse of power. Those who lead or aspire to lead in the political or corporate arenas, for example, experience a constant maneuvering for advantage.

"But what has this to do with me?" you ask. "I do not wish to be king or even president of the church council." No doubt. But each one of us has his or her own sphere of power, either in reality or in the wishes of the heart. These are our own little kingdoms, where we want to get our way and be honored by others, where we manipulate those who stand in our path or those who can help us achieve our goals. Our kingdom may be ever so small, perhaps no more than a spouse and a house or our work, but kingdom it is, and we would have it in our control so it can serve our purposes.

Consider the form of power called popularity. We want to be recognized and appreciated by others. When we are among those whose respect we covet, we instinctively tend to tilt remarks in the direction of acceptability. Perhaps we remain silent when truth is bent or join in gossip hoping that a little bad news at someone else's expense will lift our rating a notch or two. We are drawn to go along with the crowd either to gain approval or avoid disapproval. The fear of the Lord may be the beginning of wisdom, but does it vanish when we want acceptance from people whose wisdom may be attached to something else? Instead of the Lord, a few questionable friends may command our respect.

So quickly does the desire for power overpower us. And for so tiny a kingdom. Jesus said, "What good is it for you to gain the *whole world*, yet forfeit your soul?" (Mark 8:36). But we are prone to sell out for a speck of the world so insignificant as to invite laughter from fallen angels.

In the end, all power will fail except that which comes from the author of power. As others have noted, nothing is more certain than that "the powers that be" will soon become "the powers that were."

When Roman generals returned to ancient Rome as victors, they and their soldiers were given triumphal parades through the city, with music, booty, strange animals, and humiliated captives from conquered lands displayed for all to see. But the heroes were also accompanied by servants who shouted, "All glory is fleeting."

Fleeting it is, and the best that power can offer beyond some momentary advantage is the pseudo-immortality of being remembered by others. But it cannot possibly give life-transcendent meaning. Because power as an object of worship is part of the culture of death, in the end it offers nothing but weakness.

## The Corruption of Power

"Power tends to corrupt, and absolute power corrupts absolutely," wrote Lord Acton.[3] The statement is often quoted (usually in abbreviated form) because it touches a central nerve concerning power. All of us use power for selfish purposes; the greater the power, the more we are tempted to abuse it, imagining ourselves increasingly exempt from moral and legal constraints that mere mortals are expected to observe. With power comes the temptation to arrogance.

The Bible is replete with examples of the abuse of power. Nowhere is the gravitation of power toward abuse, and of abusers toward power, more cleverly presented than in the Book of Judges, chapter 9. Jotham, the youngest son of Gideon, following a murderous grab for power by an older brother, offers a parable. The trees, said Jotham, once sought a king and asked the olive tree, "Reign over us." The olive tree refused. So did the fig tree and the vine. Finally the trees asked the thornbush, and the thornbush said, "If you really want to anoint me king over you, come and take refuge in my shade" (v. 15 NIV). With a hint of the tyranny to come, the thornbush told the trees that if they did not do so, he would bring a consuming fire upon the finest of their trees—the cedars of Lebanon.

Jesus encountered opposition from those in power because he seemed to pose a threat to them—which he was, but not in the way they feared. King Herod slaughtered the male infants and toddlers of Bethlehem to make sure that "the one who has been born king of the Jews" did not survive to take his throne (Matt. 2:1–18). Later, the religious authorities in Jerusalem decided that Jesus must die so that people would not be torn away from their leadership and create an explosive hope for political deliverance that might trigger a crushing military response from the Romans. With this in mind, the high priest Caiaphas said, "It is better for you that one man die for the people than that the whole nation perish" (John 11:50). And although Pilate knew Jesus to be innocent of the charges against him, he feared that the aroused mob might touch off a riot in that tinderbox of a nation, endangering his own career; so he ordered the crucifixion. On a wholly different level, there are indications of opposition to Jesus from his own family and circle of friends, spurred in part, we may assume, by the controversy that he aroused, which proved a huge embarrassment to them (Mark 3:20–21, 31–35). Their reputations—a form of power—were on the line.

Power is readily idolized, and idols always demand more. That is true of wealth and pleasure, and it is the case with power. Carried to its extreme, the lust for power becomes an insane obsession, as we have seen in Hitler, Stalin, and Mao, each responsible for the deaths of tens of millions, and, on a lesser scale, in other tyrants even today. Power corrupted cares little about injury to others. That is the case with bullies at school, and it is true of us whenever our desires ride carelessly over the needs of others—something that happens more frequently than we realize.

The attempt to control or expand our little kingdoms leads to misunderstanding, conflict, anger, broken relations, even war. Years ago, my brother Paul's family was driving in Central America shortly after a "soccer war" had broken out between Honduras and Nicaragua (so called because a soccer match provided the spark that touched it off). One of his children asked, "Why do countries have wars?" Paul answered, "I'll tell you in a few minutes." Soon his children began to quarrel. "Now I can tell you why countries go to war," he said.

Lord Acton did not have it precisely right. It is not power that corrupts, but we who corrupt power. "All politicians are crooked," it is said. The statement, however, reveals more about the speaker than it does about politicians, because implicit is the admission, "If I were a politician, I would be crooked." Power corrupted illustrates yet again that evil represents a misuse of what is good. It is a good that each of us has, however limited in scope. It is a good that each of us also corrupts to some extent, because, as Henri Nouwen has said, "power offers an easy substitute for the hard task of love."[4] For that we need forgiveness. But we must also see, in the call to follow Jesus, his invitation to use the gift of power in a very different way.

## The Pretense of Weakness

The parable of the trees inviting the thornbush to rule over them (Judges 9) illustrates the abuse of power. But indirectly, it offers another lesson—the olive tree, the fig tree, or the vine could have accepted the same invitation. Rejecting opportunities to lead can be immoral, because power is also abused by neglect. To pretend to be powerless—to have power at our disposal and fail to use it when the well-being of others is at stake—is no less an abuse than is the bending of power to achieve our own wayward aims. One is a sin of commission, the other a sin of omission. Although our sins of commission are more visible and therefore attract more notice, our sins of omission may be more damaging. During my life, I have offended and hurt people countless times through selfish actions or thoughtless comments, but I have little doubt that the good I could have done but failed to do far exceeds my sins of commission.

That is especially true of us who live under a form of government in which power has been extensively invested in citizens. We cannot just point to officials and blame them for what is wrong, because ours is a government of and by the people. Our elected leaders will make decisions largely on the basis of the opinions we press upon them. Do poor people lack food and health insurance? Our silence has probably contributed.

"Power cannot be wielded without guilt," Reinhold Niebuhr observed, but "the disavowal of the responsibilities of power can involve an individual or nation in even more grievous guilt."[5] The text of choice is the parable of the talents in Matthew 25. It occurs in a section that groups words of Jesus about preparing for the day of judgment. The story is about three servants, each given sizable sums to invest for their master, who had gone on an extended trip abroad. When the master came home, the first two servants returned double what they had been given; the third ser-

95

vant who had buried his money in the ground, simply gave it back, along with some grousing. The master condemned that servant as wicked and lazy because he had feigned powerlessness, when in fact he had done nothing with the power he had.

The point of the story, of course, is that we are to use what God has given us to further God's work on earth, and that we will one day be called to give an account. In order to make absolutely clear what that work includes, the parable is followed immediately by the last judgment scene, in which the Son of Man says that when we help the hungry, the thirsty, the stranger, the naked, the sick, and the prisoner, we are helping him; and when we do not do those things, we turn our backs on him and will be judged accordingly. It is an awesome scene and a stunning reminder of what God expects us to do.

A few years ago, the nation learned about the death of Elisa Izquierdo, a six-year-old blind girl who was physically abused and killed by her drug-addicted mother in my old neighborhood, New York's Lower East Side. Teacher and author Jonathan Kozol noted that officeholders had cut back on basic services of life protection for poor children such as Elisa, and added:

> There is an agreeable illusion, evidenced in much of the commentary about Elisa, that those of us who witness the abuse of innocence—so long as we are standing at a certain distance—need not feel complicit in these tragedies. But this is the kind of ethical exemption that Dietrich Bonhoeffer called "cheap grace." Knowledge carries with it certain theological imperatives. The more we know, the harder it becomes to grant ourselves exemption. "Evil exists," a student in the South Bronx told me. . . . "Somebody has power. Pretending that they don't so they don't need to use it to help people— that is my idea of evil."[6]

He might have added that the "somebody" includes us, because those officeholders were elected by ordinary citizens and usually reflect their wishes.

Each of us has been given power. Each of us has influence. We can either use it to achieve the Master's purpose, or we can bury it and pretend to be helpless.

## Power Doing Good

Power is a gift of God. When God gave humans authority to rule over the earth and subdue it, real power was conferred. But power, like every other gift, was meant to honor God, not take the place of God. When we begin to love power and use it for ourselves, it becomes our master. Power is properly respected only as a gift from God used in service to God.

That does not mean relinquishing ambition, but redirecting it. "Christianity proposes not to extinguish our natural desires. It promises to bring the desires under just control and direct them to their true object,"[7] said William Wilberforce, a member of the British Parliament, who, with the help of a core of fellow evangelical Christians and eventually many others, succeeded in getting Parliament to abolish the slave trade in 1806. Wilberforce used his power as a gifted young legislator; in mobilizing public support against slavery, his influence grew. Twenty-seven years later, just four days before Wilberforce's death, Parliament voted to end slavery forever throughout the British empire, an astonishing achievement.

A more modest example of servant-power occurred in the mid 1980s, when the United Nations Children's Fund and the World Health Organization launched the "children's health revolution," which promoted a few simple, inexpensive methods to reduce what was then forty thousand daily deaths of children under the age of five from curable infections and malnutrition. Bread for the World drafted legislation that was introduced in Congress to support that campaign, and tens of thousands of ordinary citizens began writing to their representatives in the U.S. House and Senate, urging its passage. Congress enacted the bill and continues to appropriate several hundred million dollars a year for child survival. In no small part because of those letters, by the turn of the century ten thousand fewer children died each day. Much remains to be done, but the progress shows how even so small a step as a letter from an ordinary voter to an elected official can have the effect of saving lives.

The highest expression of servant leadership is Jesus himself (Phil. 2:6–11). His disciples, however, were not eager to learn this. Just as they began the journey to Jerusalem where Jesus would be crucified, James and John asked (discreetly through their mother) to receive the positions of highest rank in his kingdom—a request that angered the other disciples. Jesus called the twelve together and said (to paraphrase), "In the world rulers love to lord it over others. But that's not the way it is going to be among you. Whoever wants to be great must be your servant, and whoever wants to be first must be your slave—just as I did not come to be served but to serve and give my life as a ransom for others" (Matt. 20:20–28). On the eve of his crucifixion, Jesus took a basin of water and did the lowly, grubby kindness of washing his disciples' feet—an example, he said, of how we are called to serve one another.

As Jesus demonstrated, servant power may appear as weakness, but it is the only power that has a place in the kingdom, and the only power that endures. The ultimate paradox is that Jesus, utterly crushed and helpless on the cross, became the resurrected Lord; the powers that crushed him were reduced to unflattering footnotes. Subsequently, the news of Christ's victory became the power of God for salvation, a power that is at work in us now through the Holy Spirit. It is almost impossible to read the writings of the New Testament—Acts, or Ephesians 1 and 2, for example—and not be struck by the sense of power that filled members of the marginal sect that sprang up in the wake of Jesus' death and resurrection.

In addition, the apostle Paul asserts that God's power is made perfect through human weakness, including our suffering. That is a great encouragement to people like myself with limited gifts and a shy disposition, for it tells me that God can use even the little that I have to do great good when it is offered in his service.

Two seemingly opposite themes merge in the word "service." Both human power and human weakness are to be offered in service, and God uses each to accomplish his purpose in Christ. Joseph, Moses, Esther, and President Lincoln are examples of people who used positions of power for servant leadership. The prophet Nathan, Jeremiah, Mary, St. Francis, Martin Luther King, Jr., and Mother Teresa exemplify those who led, at least initially, from positions of relative weakness placed at God's disposal. These are heroic models. But their example tells us that in small and ordinary ways, God can use what we offer, no matter how powerless or influential we may be.

I think of the Coverstons—Paul is a laborer and Linda a preschool teacher. They volunteer faithfully in the church, are raising two adopted children, and exemplify the desire to make all aspects of their life an offering to God.

I think of Carolyn Long, who spent two years as a Peace Corps volunteer in Africa, and then a decade serving Inter-Action, an organization for private U.S. agencies working in developing countries. Now a mother, she continues to use her leadership both within and outside the church for advocacy against hunger and poverty.

I think of Charlie and Gloria Jacobs. A retired hospital financial director, Charlie became a Third Order Franciscan almost fifty years ago, when he was inspired by St. Francis to embrace a life of simplicity and concern for the poor.

Gloria has been a hospital volunteer for most of her life, while Charlie spends much of his energy assisting and advocating on behalf of hungry people.

In a setting as small as a family, as varied as those with whom we work and socialize, or as far-reaching as a community halfway around the world, our acts of kindness and our prayers may affect a thousand or a million lives in future generations.

Power used selfishly is power corrupted. Ability buried is power wasted. But opportunity to do good, received as a trust from God and exercised to help others, is power ennobled.

# EIGHT

# Faces of Affluence

Economics may confuse or bore you, but much of our life is shaped not only by our own use of money, but also by the way others, including companies, governments, and individuals, use it. That makes economics a spiritual as well as a material concern. So we need to look briefly at several economic issues.[1]

## Consumerism

Books and articles on simplified living come down hard on consumer buying, and with good reason. Materialism is almost synonymous with excessive consumption and an upward-spiraling demand for products and services, the need for which is artificially stimulated by advertising. Advertising prompts us to want things. That some people buy advertised products increases the desire of others who are now doubly attracted by what they see—first on television and then around town or among colleagues. In this way, the lust for possessions, made more accessible by easy credit, begins to consume our time and energy, blinding us to the needs of others.

But wait. The above diagnosis contains a couple of major omissions that indicate a highly positive side to growth and consumption. First, inventions and discoveries that lie behind economic growth have lifted much of humankind out of grinding poverty; they are, in considerable part, the fruit of the revolutionary biblical view of creation as distinct from the Creator, and therefore a fit object of investigation. Inventions and discoveries have also been stimulated by the Judeo-Christian belief that history is moving not in endless repetitive cycles, but toward the fulfillment of God's purposes. We may confidently believe that God takes great joy in seeing life enhanced for so many.

Second, poor people no less than others depend upon economic growth for opportunities to get ahead. Economic growth since the Industrial Revolution dramatically reduced poverty, first in Europe and North America, and then throughout the rest of the world. Even in the poorest countries, education and health have improved. Growth has benefited some people much more than others and widened the gap between rich and poor. But without economic growth, more people become poor, and the poor become even poorer. So if our stand against materialism and consumption is made in the interests of poor people, we seem to be on shaky ground. To condemn growing consumption is to oppose an economic force that has brought vast improvement to our lives and greatly reduced poverty.

The case against materialism must be more nuanced and spiritually grounded. Consumption, it turns out, is a mixed bag, neither all good nor all bad. We get some indication of this from the Bible, whose writers condemn the accumulation of wealth but also speak of prosperity as a blessing. "Humility and fear of the LORD bring wealth and honor and life" (Prov. 22:4 NIV). The apostle Paul writes to the

Christians in Philippi that he has learned to be content whether living with plenty or living in want (Phil. 4:10–13). He doesn't seek deprivation, nor does he despise "plenty." And he does not condemn money, either, though another letter warns against the *love* of money, "a root of all kinds of evil" that causes some to wander from the faith and bring grief upon themselves (1 Tim. 6:10).

Consider, also, that throughout the Bible (the Psalms in particular) we are urged to praise God for creation and to give thanks for God's generosity in providing for us. Far from evoking shame, God's bounty is supposed to be celebrated. However, it is to be celebrated in community and shared with others: the poor, the crippled, and the blind, who Jesus said (Luke 14:12–21) are unable to repay. In contrast to John the Baptizer, Jesus enjoyed wining and dining with others, including those socially despised. His critics said, "Here is a glutton and a drunkard, a friend of tax collectors and 'sinners'" (Luke 7:34). It was not a compliment.

The issue of what and how much to consume is complex. If life belongs totally to God, who blesses us with material gifts, we need to use and enjoy them faithfully. How can we do that?

The question invites not casual responses, but a searching of the heart. It touches not only personal habits, but also public policies concerning the use of the nation's wealth. That leads us to examine a driving force behind national and personal prosperity: free enterprise capitalism.

## Capitalism

My affluence and yours, the nation's affluence, and our consumption-oriented culture—all of them—are tied to free enterprise. Free enterprise has proven to be a remarkable engine for economic growth and for its ability to stimulate the kind of innovation that can expand opportunities and improve lives. Think of telephones, cars, airplanes, food, farm technology, and medical progress. That these advances generate jobs on a large scale further benefits entire populations. Who can doubt that this kind of material progress is part of the "everything" in the earth that belongs to the Lord (Ps. 24:1) and that we are commanded to take care of and utilize?

For all the good it can do, however, free enterprise capitalism has grave defects. These defects gave plausibility to that woefully misguided venture called communism and, more recently in the Islamic world, to radical ideas about imposing strict Islamic law on societies. Capitalism stimulates and thrives on our human desire to possess more, a desire that instinctively gravitates toward greed, which tends to create disparities that make some rich, while leaving many impoverished. It is good at generating wealth, not so good at spreading it around. A related defect is that free enterprise does not distinguish between selling Bibles and selling drugs or sex. It is simply driven by the profit motive. There is nothing wrong with profit if it is obtained honestly and justly and used in a godly way. But the profit motive appeals to our acquisitive nature. It nourishes greed and can make us callous to the suffering of others. In short, the genius of free enterprise is also its central problem.

Left to its own devices, free enterprise capitalism would ruin the environment and let people starve. As a result, no nation leaves free enterprise entirely on its own. Every country will devise policies that, at least to some extent, guide free enterprise toward serving the wider public good, in this way acknowledging that while free enterprise may be a remarkable engine for driving economic growth, an engine is not the same as a steering wheel.

Every one of the fifty United States offers free public education and requires school attendance at least through the age of sixteen. Despite shortcomings, that policy helps to equalize opportunity and prepare young people to participate productively in the U.S. economy. By itself, free enterprise would not do this. But the public has decided to spread some of its wealth to all citizens through education, to the benefit of everyone, including private enterprise, which is rewarded with better trained and more innovative workers and leaders.

Another example of giving free enterprise guidance is legislation that taxes high incomes at a higher rate than low incomes. Environmental regulations aim at limiting pollution of air, land, and water, and at restoring them from damage already done. Roads, police and fire protection, and a host of other tax-supported services help businesses as well as individuals. Safety nets, such as food stamps and Medicaid in the United States, universal health care in Europe and Canada, and social security in all of these, ensure at least some basic provision for people who otherwise might be trampled to death by a system driven solely by profits.

Ironically, the success of free enterprise capitalism depends upon moral values, such as honesty and compassion, that are borrowed from elsewhere. Without such supporting values, free enterprise (or any other economic system) would eventually self-destruct through its own excesses.

To work its magic for the economy, free enterprise needs plenty of room and not too many restraints. But to achieve public justice, free enterprise, like the urge to consume, needs to be tamed and guided. That requires a delicate balance, one that is endlessly debated, but which touches the central nerve of justice—not justice as an abstract idea, but as basic opportunity for children and others whose lives frequently hang in the balance.

That kind of justice is an affair of the soul for each of us. But people of means have a special obligation before God to ensure justice for those who are poor and vulnerable. With greater affluence comes corresponding responsibility to make sure that a system that has been generous to oneself is also generous to others.

## The Moral Ambiguity of Affluence

Widespread economic gains have modified our understanding of affluence. First, poverty and affluence are relative terms. Poverty in the United States or Western Europe, for example, usually includes goods, services, and purchasing power that poor people in developing countries can't begin to imagine. King Louis XIV had no modern plumbing, electricity, or central heat in the Palace of Versailles; nor did he have television, an automobile, or access to modern medical care. In this respect, he lagged way behind most poor people in France or the United States two centuries later. Yet no one would consider this man of immense wealth economically poor. The extent to which things are generally available makes a big difference in how we determine what is affluence or poverty.

Second, affluence has spread to many people through gains in production. In biblical times most people were peasants. They tilled the land and raised livestock, usually living at a subsistence or near-subsistence level. If the rains came and war did not, they had enough. The royalty, by contrast, could accumulate wealth through conquest and royal taxation. Some others could also live in relative luxury through the private accumulation of land and slaves. Such wealth usually got passed along to future generations through inheritance. One way or another, if people got rich, they ordinarily did so at the expense of others, by taking what others produced. This fact weighed heavily in shaping biblical views of wealth and poverty.

Today, however, the situation has changed. Dramatic growth in the world's economic output (from perhaps one or two trillion dollars in 1900 to $37 trillion in 2000) largely represents the creation of new wealth and widely distributed wealth.[2] As a result, most of the world's population has at least some access to material goods and services that previously, if available, would have been restricted to the rich.

106

Most of this change occurred since the Industrial Revolution and the emergence of democratic governments beginning in the late eighteenth century. The Industrial Revolution generated injustices of its own—low wages, long hours, terrible working conditions, child labor, urban slums, unemployment, and many related social problems. Despite grave inequities, however, technological and social engineering has made it possible for vast numbers of people to raise their standard of living to levels that could only have been dreamed about a few generations ago.

God must be delighted when children can go to school, prepare themselves for jobs and careers, be well nourished and clothed, and live in homes that are warm in the winter. Surely God wants us to make the individual and social effort necessary to maintain or to achieve such economic well-being for ourselves, our families, and others within the nation and throughout the world. Just as surely, God does not want us to bask in affluence while others starve.

Today prosperity is to a great extent being created rather than taken from others, and many are able to become part of the creation and enjoyment of prosperity. This must be taken into account when applying biblical admonitions to people of the twenty-first century. Affluence, at least in moderation, is today more often defensible as a blessing and is less often in violation of others than was the case in biblical times.

There is, however, a darker side to all of this. In tracing the history of Western values, Lewis Mumford described a huge shift that accompanied industrialism and consumerism. Except for sloth, the seven deadly sins were recast as virtues. "Greed, envy, gluttony, and pride became driving forces of the new economy. . . . Unbounded power was harnessed to equally unbounded appetites."[3] That should arouse suspicion.

Our growing affluence makes mammon an ever more attractive idol. For one thing, we can become so engrossed in getting things for our "unbounded appetites" that we lose sight of life's purpose and the truly desperate plight of others. For another, the factors that contribute to the world's improvement (such as hard work, efficiency, complex organizations, and the desire to make the most of life) often lead to distortions in our personal lives that leave insufficient room for prayer, play, love, and generosity. The same factors have also generated waste and environmental degradation on an alarming scale.

All of this compels us to understand God's expectations for us under circumstances that are different and more complex than they were two thousand years ago.

Like the Sabbath, the economy was made for people, not people for the economy, and we do well to put people first. God has given us what Wendell Berry calls "the Great Economy" of nature, within which is the little industrial economy of our human construction; but we tend to make the latter the *only* economy.[4] Berry's "Great Economy" is God's economy. Appropriately, the New Testament word for stewardship is *oikonomia*, from which the English word *economy* derives. God is the Great Steward, and we are to imitate his stewardship—one of utmost care, generosity, and love. That is a high challenge. But for a Christian, working to achieve a public justice that more nearly reflects God's stewardship is part of the call to discipleship.

## Those Left Behind

Stimulated by computer technology, our global economy has greatly increased global income. Advancement for some, however, can be the cause of poverty for others. Corporate executives may enrich themselves at the expense of poorly paid and poorly treated workers. An industrial plant may relocate, benefiting stockholders, but leaving behind a community of unemployed people.

On the whole, the expanding economy has created more beneficiaries than victims, more winners than losers. Even so, it has disproportionately benefited those who are already prosperous, while leaving much of the world poor. In doing so, the gap between rich and poor people, as well as the gap between rich and poor countries, has widened more than ever. The rich get richer and most of the poor stay that way.

In his landmark study, *The Wealth and Poverty of Nations*, historian and economist David S. Landes concludes that "the big challenge and threat is the gap in wealth and health that separates rich and poor." He calls that gap "the greatest single problem and danger facing the world of the Third Millennium."[5]

How big is the gap? Landes estimates that the difference in average income per person between industrialized Switzerland and nonindustrialized Mozambique is about four hundred to one. Two hundred and fifty years ago the gap between the richest country and the poorest country was about five to one, and the difference between Europe and China or India, about two to one or less.[6]

Within the United States, the gap between rich and poor people widened during the last two decades of the twentieth century. During this period of substantial economic growth, the richest segments of society benefited by far the most, while the poorest segments either fell behind or showed little gain. And although it is true that poor people in the U.S. had more appliances than was the case a generation earlier, they did not have more food, because ability to buy enough food for a minimally adequate diet is the key measurement used to determine the poverty line in the United States. In 2000, eight million Americans were classified as hungry, and another twenty-three million as at risk of hunger, which meant that they had to skimp on food or skip meals.[7]

Barbara Ehrenreich, a Ph.D., wondered what it would be like to live on low wages. She left her Florida home and tested the idea in various parts of the country, working as a waitress, for example, or a cleaning woman. She reported her experience in *Nickled and Dimed: On (Not) Getting by in America*.[8] There were plenty of low-paying jobs, and even more indignity, but she often had to work more than one job at a time to survive, and she had only herself to support. Think of all the janitors, nursing home attendants, and hotel maids who support children on wages that can hardly sustain one person.

Where the historian, economist, and inquisitive writer stop, the Lord of history speaks. The word from the Bible is both encouraging and alarming. It tells us that God's bounty may indeed be received with thanksgiving, but with the blessing comes accountability. Part of that accountability is an obligation to share with great generosity so that those without basic necessities will also have a place at the table.

# NINE

# How Much Is Enough?

Nelson Rockefeller, an heir to the Rockefeller fortune, was once asked, "How much is enough?" Rockefeller paused for a moment, smiled and replied, "Just a little bit more." It was an honest answer. Whether we are rich or poor, one thing we can never seem to get is enough. Because idols appear to work, though never to the satisfaction of the heart, they constantly induce us to want "just a little bit more."

When twenty-year-old Venus Williams added the U.S. Open tennis championship and eight hundred thousand dollars to a string of victories, President Clinton congratulated her by phone. After they exchanged a few pleasantries, she said, "Me and my accountant, sometimes we have a tough time because I don't want to pay my taxes. . . . Can you lower my taxes? I work so hard, Mr. President."[1] A prayer for more.

Turn-of-the-century analyses of newly emerging shapers of culture in the United States noted trends toward status based on consumption, greater insistence on freedom of choice in everything from fashion to morality, a growing inclination to consider all truth-claims matters of personal preference, and preoccupation with pleasure and comfort.[2] This may describe a paradise of sorts, but not exactly the satisfaction that comes through sacrifice or the crown of life beyond the cross.

Older people are wooed by messages proclaiming the virtues of retirement with comfort. Nothing wrong with that. But marginal comfort and enjoyment for myself easily get to be more important than survival for others. These comforts easily *become* my life and begin to define my purpose for being.

People want "more" in order to be happier. Numerous studies have shown that when the "more" means moving from deprivation to having adequate food, shelter, clothing, health care, and a few amenities, happiness does substantially increase. Beyond that point, however, additional income contributes very little to people's sense of well-being, though they imagine it will contribute much. Once you have met basic needs, the extras don't add much happiness, and not infrequently they detract from it by nurturing a habit of desire that breeds dissatisfaction. David Steindl-Rast and Sharon Lebell observe, "The economics of affluence demands that things that were special for us last year must now be taken for granted."[3] And things taken for granted do not evoke gratitude, which is the core of happiness.

My grandparents began farming two hundred mostly wooded acres in Wisconsin in 1899, where they raised nine children, including my father. They lived largely on their own crops and livestock, though my grandmother's records show a cash income in 1902 of $532.14 (worth much more, of course, in today's dollars). They were generous with what they had and did not consider themselves poor. If *they* had enough, does that set a standard for us? We recoil at the thought. But is the alternative simply to keep pace with ever-rising standards of affluence?

How much is enough? Formulas elude us, yet our answer has far-reaching effects on ourselves and others. The question invites additional questions. How much of what? One can, for example, distinguish between junk food and good nutrition, for the mind and spirit as well as the body. In relation to what alternatives? Human needs surround us and have some claim upon us. Above all, what is God's purpose for us? And is my "enough" helping to fulfill that purpose? Does it help me celebrate and share God's love? The questions reflect the age-old internal struggle between sin and obedience.

"Why settle for more and miss the best?" Tom Sine asks. Why not choose a life that counts, he suggests, enjoy it more, and share what you have? Less can be part of something infinitely better than the pursuit of more.[4]

"Give us this day our daily bread," we pray, asking not simply for food, but for all that we need to support this body and life. As part of Jesus' prayer for the coming of God's gracious rule in our lives, this simple request casts a much wider net than we may suppose. It is a prayer for enough, a prayer for trust that God will provide whatever is necessary. We are afraid to let go, afraid we will lose things we love too much—exactly the problem. Both rich and poor prisoners of mammon participate in the myth of scarcity, so for them there is never enough. But by trusting, we shed anxiety about our needs and no longer covet excess. That is a great freedom. We can then receive God's "enough" with gratitude that moves us to share all we can with others so that they, too, may experience God's "enough"; for in praying "give *us* this day our daily bread," we seek bread not just for ourselves but for others as well. That points us toward the common good and away from lonely acquisition.

## Staying behind the Joneses

Call it the Joneses syndrome. We see what people a notch or two more affluent than ourselves have, and we begin to want it, too. Like forbidden fruit, it looks too good to resist. So we find ourselves on a treadmill, keeping up with the Joneses only to find that the Joneses (who are keeping up with other Joneses) are constantly upping the ante so that we never quite reach the point of satisfaction. In reality, of course, we seldom fasten on one particular family, but on our broader social surroundings.

The psychology behind the Joneses syndrome is as simple as family life. A child does not expect an ice cream bar for lunch. But if a sibling gets one, then having an ice cream bar suddenly seems not just desirable but a dire necessity. A child does not instinctively long for a particular brand or style of sneakers. But if "everyone" in his class starts wearing them and commenting on those who don't, lack of those sneakers makes him feel deprived and inferior. Kids want what other kids have. In this respect, they are strikingly like adults. Psychologist David G. Myers writes that this is a big part of the reason most people in the industrialized world, living with comforts unknown to wealthy families in earlier generations, do not consider themselves wealthy.[5]

Our habit of comparing ourselves to others may explain why it is that "if you escape poverty your happiness increases, yet, paradoxically, societies do not become happier as they progress from relative poverty to affluence."[6] Polls show that even the rich seldom consider themselves rich, because they tend to define "rich" as those earning more than they do. Myers notes that when the Oakland Athletics signed outfielder Jose Canseco to a $4.7 million annual salary, Rickey Henderson, his fellow outfielder, refused to show up for spring training, complaining that his $3 million contract was unfair. The same thing happens to the most devout. Writer Gerard Straub, on pilgrimage in Italy, stayed for a

few days in a hermitage that St. Francis frequented for solitude. He almost panicked trying to adjust to his cramped
cell. Then he learned that the other cells were even smaller.
"Suddenly," he writes, "this small room seems like a suite."[7]

Which Joneses are we trying to keep up with? Almost
always the Joneses who are ahead of us. Perhaps we should
stay behind those Joneses and compare ourselves with the
Joneses who lack food, clothing, and medical care. When
I visited Vietnam a few years after the war, families in Hanoi
lived in cramped quarters and each household was allowed
only one 15-watt bulb. I no longer think of electricity in a
casual way. People there were desperately poor, like the
young man I saw staring into a store window. He caught my
attention because his shirt was so threadbare that separate
parts of it were held together by wires. I took his picture—
but failed to give him my shirt. So large is the gap between
observation and commitment. Still, he helps me remember
a different set of Joneses.

We may be most heavily engaged in keeping up with the
Joneses when we are least aware of doing so, because we are
so busy reaching for a synthetic sense of self. To take pride
in our latest purchases is evidence not simply of insecurity
but of a misplaced identity. All the more pathetic for those
who truly believe they are children of God and eternal heirs
of the kingdom. If we believe this, why should we behave
like planetary orphans? And if we do not establish a solid
basis for resisting such pressures, our children will almost
certainly be swallowed up by them. A clear sense of who we
are, our purpose in life, and a self-confidence anchored in
God enable us to reject the tinsel of status and opt instead
for the real thing.

If keeping up with the Joneses is chasing the wind, stay-
ing behind them is hardly a transcendent goal, either. Infinitely better to put our lives at God's disposal. Pointing to
the awesome mercy of God, Paul urges us to become living
sacrifices to God. Instead of conforming to the world, we

115

can be transformed in Christ (Rom. 12:1–2). But that kind of counter-cultural courage requires knowing who we are and acting accordingly.

## No Easy Answers

If only God would give us a simple way to determine how much is enough! For some the answer is the tithe. But tithing is beyond the reach of many, and it suggests to others that if God gets 10 percent the rest is ours to do with as we please. Because all of "ours" belongs to God, God asks us to submit all of it in obedient service. Our job is to do that as faithfully as possible.

But what does that mean? What kind of house should my family live in? How much should we spend on cars, appliances, clothing, and recreation? And what about education, bicycles, music lessons, or use of the phone? Money is a consideration in all of these, but so is the use of time and talent. And how do we weigh the needs and wants of our family in relation to the needs of those who are desperately poor? The difficulty of answering these questions lies not only in their complexity, but also in our waywardness. We instinctively think of ourselves in these matters, but Jesus has told us to love our neighbors with the same kind of instinctive concern. Doing so is not easy.

The question came up in our home, should we have rugs? Rugs are not essential, but they protect the floor, provide some warmth, and reduce the creaking that wakes my wife when I rise early in the morning. So we compromised: some rugs and some bare floors. I also think of a friend who supports his family by laying rugs, a reminder that buying rugs is related to employment for many people. Since there is no clear case to be made for or against the purchase of rugs, one guideline might look like this: when considering whether or not to spend money on nonessentials, ask whether doing so enables us to live more fully for God and people in need, including family.

When my daughter Leah was thirteen years old, she asked if she could get a manicure "just this once." It was her money and she had always been generous with it, so I said, "Yes." When I went to the shop to pick her up, I learned that it cost twenty-five dollars, and commented on that with some astonishment. "Am I in trouble?" she asked. "No," I told her, "but we need to talk about it." We did, and in the course of the conversation she decided to contribute an equal amount for hunger relief. But how do you use a situation like that to foster a desire to follow Jesus without being legalistic or seeming to cut a 50/50 deal with God?

I have come to view some of my own decisions about money differently. For many years, I lived in an old tenement apartment on New York's Lower East Side. The highest rent I paid was fifty-four dollars a month. But the rent was low mainly because of a rent-control law. At the time, I supported rent control as a protection for the poor (not to mention my own advantage). Today I believe that law, enacted during World War II, should have been phased out long ago, because it reduced incentives for the upkeep of buildings and the construction of new housing. Over the long haul, it has probably done more harm than good to poor people.

I gave away part of the royalties of my first book, *Faces of Poverty*, to the poor, but—with qualms of conscience for doing so—put most of it in a savings account "just in case." As it turned out, a few years later that savings allowed me to do some research and writing on hunger, which led to the founding of Bread for the World. The savings supported my wife and first child for several years and made possible the launching of a Christian citizens' movement against hunger. The money was there at least partly because of my selfishness. But how much "just in case" money is okay and at what point does it violate discipleship? There is no pat answer, of course. A friend tells me, "We should keep bringing decisions to God and be open to investing in the development of our gifts so we can do more good."

Bread for the World began on a financial shoestring, so we adopted the policy of paying people on the basis of need rather than position, which meant some support personnel earned more than a few department directors and I did. The policy served well for a dozen years or so, but as Bread for the World's staff expanded, it became increasingly difficult to administer in a fair and consistent way. And although we developed a highly committed and professionally able staff, sometimes the policy prevented us from hiring exceptional candidates for key positions. One of the things I did before stepping aside as president was to help obtain a modification of that policy so that positions are now more nearly in line with market realities. Many staff members vigorously opposed higher salaries (!) because it seemed to them a betrayal of principle. But Bread's mission had to drive this decision. Our salary policy had to enhance that mission.

Even so, my successor, David Beckmann, who was having a promising career at the World Bank, took about a two-thirds cut in salary in order to assume the leadership of what is now the nation's premier lobby against hunger. He did not sell everything he had and give it to the poor. Yet he and his family put all that they had, including enormous energy and talent, in service to this work of God on behalf of poor and hungry people. Is that not what Jesus had in mind?

Variations and changing circumstances defy prescriptive answers. The economy of Judea in the first century was vastly different from today's industrial economies. The absence of microwaves and toilets that flush then does not necessarily rule them out for us now. I belong to a church body that once opposed life insurance as a violation of Jesus' command not to worry about tomorrow. Family situations and personal needs differ enormously. Exceptional job responsibilities may require homes with amenities that are not needed for most of us. And life for all of us was meant to be a celebration of God's generosity, not a set of stringent rules. Allowing for these things, it is also true that we have an uncanny ability to rationalize our advantages, forget the suffering of others, skim lightly over the words of the prophets and of Jesus, and become prisoners of our own interests.

Each of us has to decide what to do with what we have. With the best of intentions our decisions are flawed, so we live always by grace. But those decisions will be more nearly in conformity with God's purpose for us if we faithfully seek that purpose and have love as our aim.

Jim Elliot, who along with four missionary companions was killed in an attempt to bring the gospel to the Auca Indians of Ecuador, had this as part of his personal creed: "He is no fool who gives what he cannot keep to gain what he cannot lose."[8] It is a sound principle also when deciding how much is enough.

## The Bible on Possessions

Christians turn to the Bible for guidance only to discover not one, but several views regarding possessions. This should come as no surprise, because the Bible was written over a period of centuries by many authors who reflected widely diverse circumstances. Proverbs, attributed to King Solomon, for example, would hardly be expected to sound like the thunder of the prophet Amos against the abuse of wealth and power. In addition, most Christians understand that the Bible unfolds God's revelation to us progressively until at last God's message arrives personally in Jesus of Nazareth.

Biblical writers, for example, wrestled with the question of whether personal calamity was a judgment of God against sin. The Book of Job eloquently addressed this issue, but the disciples of Jesus reflected the prevailing view when they asked concerning the man born blind, "Who sinned, this man or his parents . . . ?" "Neither," said Jesus (John 9:2–3).

119

In a similar way, biblical writers struggled with the relation between wealth and faith. If prosperity is the reward of faithfulness, they often asked, then why do the wicked prosper and the righteous suffer?

Three basic views about possessions emerged in the Old Testament. The first promised prosperity if people worshiped God alone and obeyed God's law. The psalmist writes, "Happy are those who fear the LORD. . . . Wealth and riches are in their houses" (Ps. 112:1, 3 NRSV). The law of Moses reflects a similar view.

> You will again obey the LORD and follow all his commands. . . . Then the LORD your God will make you most prosperous in all the work of your hands and in the fruit of your womb, the young of your livestock and the crops of your land.
>
> **DEUTERONOMY 30:8–9 NIV'**

A second, "balanced" view espoused neither wealth nor poverty, as Proverbs 30:8–9 indicates:

> Give me neither poverty nor riches,
>     but give me only my daily bread.
> Otherwise, I may have too much and disown you. . . .
> Or I may become poor and steal.
>
> **NIV**

A third view, highlighted by the prophets, denounced the amassing of wealth at the expense of the poor and urged both charity and justice as the only path consistent with allegiance to God.

At first glance, these viewpoints appear to be in conflict, and no doubt they reflect internal debate. Prosperity, however, meant not wallowing in excess, but being able to satisfy every need—a good harvest and enough to eat for the year. The blessing of prosperity was offered primarily to the people as a whole, rather than to individuals. The land belonged to the Lord (Lev. 25:23; Deut. 10:14), and the people prospered or suffered together with the conditions of nature. God's generosity was meant for the common good, as a network of laws—including division of land, tithes, gleaning, Sabbath, and jubilee justice—required. Repeated admonitions to help the poor supported this, as did warnings against taking personal credit for prosperity. The "balanced" view of seeking neither riches nor poverty is close to the "prosperity" view, though it is clear that the proverbs associated with Solomon's court tilted toward seeing prosperity in more grandiose terms and as evidence of virtue. The prophets' warnings, on the other hand, addressed the abuse of wealth.

More remarkable than the diversity in these views, then, is an underlying unity that featured fidelity to the covenant, with trust that God would give people what they needed if they were faithful and obedient.

Of the three perspectives, Jesus clearly reflected the prophetic stance with his scathing rebuke of mammon worship and the way he entered the lives of the despised poor. Recall: You cannot serve God and possessions. A camel can pass through a needle's eye more easily than a rich person can enter the kingdom. Give all that you have to the poor. Unless you give up everything, you cannot be my disciple. Jesus said these things and much more in calling for radical generosity to the poor.

Though he asked for everything, Jesus also gave everything, and what he gave was infinitely more than what he asked for. It was pure grace, pure love on his part, stopping at nothing to reclaim us and bring us home to the Father. So his request for "everything" was not legalistic, and he showed this in many ways: in forgiving, in accepting rejected people, in honoring Zacchaeus as a child of the kingdom, in eating and drinking with sinners, and in doing good on the Sabbath even when it violated rules regarded as unbreakable.

121

Writer Marva Dawn has noted that when Jesus said to store up treasures in heaven, because "where your treasure is, there your heart will be also" (Luke 12:34), he was offering a promise: give away more, and your heart will expand.[10]

The question, then, is not how much we have, but what we do with what we have. This is first and foremost a question of the heart.

## Our Calling

When Jesus said, "Sell your possessions and give to the poor" (Luke 12:33) and, "Any of you who do not give up everything you have cannot be my disciples" (Luke 14:33), was he exaggerating to make a point? Was he proposing an ideal against which our lives might be measured knowing that few of his followers would live up to it? Was it a request meant only for the most ardent inner circle of believers? Or perhaps a command given in view of an expectation that the kingdom would fully come in a very short time?

Let's admit it: Jesus was asking all who follow him to give up everything—to acknowledge that it belongs to God and must be given back to God. It is not ours to possess. That's just the way it is in the kingdom. But the *way* in which life and possessions are given to God differs widely. For some, it means literally selling all and giving the money to the poor. For most of us, Jesus gives no such directive other than repeated indications that the poor are to be uppermost in our consideration.[11] Either way, *everything* is to be given up in following Christ. The words of Jesus are not obscure, but they scare us, defy our impulses, and are difficult to manage, so we tend to ignore them or interpret them the way we wish they had been said. Dietrich Bonhoeffer describes it this way:

> If a father sends his child to bed, the boy knows at once what he has to do. But suppose he has picked up a smattering of pseudo-theology. In that case he would argue more

or less like this: "Father tells me to go to bed, but he really means that I am tired, and he does not want me to be tired. I can overcome my tiredness just as well if I go out and play. Therefore though father tells me to go to bed, he really means: 'Go out and play.'"[12]

*How* we offer everything to God, however, may depend on our calling. The New Testament gives some indication of this by its use of the word *disciple*, referring sometimes to the inner circle of the Twelve, sometimes to close followers not limited to the Twelve, and sometimes to all believers. Other clues are the "different kinds of gifts" and "different kinds of service" (1 Cor. 12:4–5) recognized in the early church. All are called to faith in Christ, but within the community of faith, people have differing gifts and some have special callings—as pastors, teachers, or missionaries, for example. And some, like the rich young man, are called to sell everything and give to the poor.

In response to that call, many of the earliest Christians in Jerusalem sold their possessions and gave to those in need. Later, as the church grew throughout the Roman empire and beyond, religious orders sprang up attracting those willing to take vows of poverty, chastity, and obedience. Often this involved a life of seclusion in a monastery or convent, but it also led St. Francis and others to go from place to place serving the poor and preaching the good news (in effect making the entire world their monastery). Francis, it should be noted, after renouncing his life of privilege and pleasure, chose a life of poverty that was more austere than that of Jesus himself; Francis was not alone in doing so. This suggests that Jesus did not prescribe the same way for everyone to offer everything.

In our day, as well, many choose to give up possessions and live in voluntary poverty in order to serve the poor. Most of them do so quietly and without fanfare. And countless more, though not selling their possessions, have seri-

123

ously attempted to put everything they have in service to Christ and his poor. Young people, for example, may choose service careers, such as teaching or parenting, rather than lucrative professions. In doing so they put *being* above *having*, and God above mammon.

I think of my neighbors, Charles and Lydia Cade, who are full of love and good works. They live in a small house, which also serves on Sundays as a chapel. Lydia (with Charles) has homeschooled their seven children, the oldest of whom is now in college on an academic scholarship. The Cades have foregone affluence to invest themselves heavily in rearing children who do not copy the culture but follow Christ. I have no doubt that a rich harvest will come from this.

Ron and Arbutus Sider live by choice in a racially mixed low-income neighborhood in Philadelphia. Ron got his Ph.D. in history at Yale and eventually became a professor at Eastern Baptist Seminary. But along the way, he was struck by the biblical witness about God's love for the poor, and he and Arbutus began to change their stewardship in response to world poverty. Ron wrote an article for a Christian campus magazine advocating a graduated tithe, starting at 10 percent for low incomes, but increasing as income rises. The article attracted attention and led to his writing a book, *Rich Christians in an Age of Hunger*,[13] which has challenged a generation of Christians to rethink their lives in relation to Christ and poor people. Sider also helped found Evangelicals for Social Action, an organization that he continues to lead. Taking the Bible seriously not only changed life for the Siders, but led to steps that have changed life for countless others, as well.

Our callings differ. But all of us are invited by Jesus to offer up all that we have and "follow me."

## The Grace of Giving

We must become receivers before we can give, and what we receive far exceeds what we are asked to give.

124

One gift of the kingdom is to restore us to our true purpose in life, and part of that purpose is using whatever we have to serve others, for to receive grace is also to show grace to others. That is the gist of what the apostle Paul wrote (2 Cor. 8:1–9), when he cited the extraordinary generosity of the Macedonian Christians toward the impoverished believers in Judea. He praised their giving as an "act of grace" (v. 6). Our grace is always a derivative grace that flows from the heart of God through Christ to us, and then from us to others. The grace of giving is dependent upon a grace received; but once received, it instinctively embraces others.

The grace of giving takes many different forms, and it is not limited to financial contributions. Time, energy, and ability are often gifts of greater value. They include such things as reading books to children, assisting the homeless, the sick, and the elderly, and helping children discover the joy of helping others. One of my tasks at Bread for the World was to raise funds from donors capable of giving large amounts. I did not take to it naturally and I never got very good at it; a colleague on staff told me to think of fund-raising as a ministry, a way of enabling people to put their lives to better use for others. "You are doing them a favor," he said. That gave me a new understanding and made an otherwise distasteful job one that brought fulfillment. I still keep in touch by phone with dozens of people who plan to leave part or all of their usually modest estates to Bread for the World when they die, just to thank them and pray for those who face special challenges.

In giving, the poor often humble the rest of us. Low-income people in the United States consistently contribute a higher percentage of their income to charity than do those who have middle or high incomes. Jesus noted an instance of this when he saw a widow put two copper coins, worth about a penny, in the temple treasury. She gave more than the rich, he said, because out of her poverty she gave everything that she had (Luke 21:1–4). She exemplified the grace of giving.

This having been said, many people of means also exemplify the grace of giving. The women who helped support Jesus and his disciples as they traveled from town to village did so (Luke 8:1–3). Philemon and others whose homes became house churches for the earliest believers showed their generosity. Gerry Haworth, an executive from Michigan, transformed Bread for the World's dilapidated office with seven hundred thousand dollars' worth of fine furniture. Millard and Linda Fuller gave away their fortune, founded Habitat for Humanity, and have enlisted thousands of volunteers around the world to build durable homes for people living in shanties. I don't know if the Fullers still live in a simple Georgia house with no air-conditioning, but it hardly matters, for they are clearly pouring their lives out for others and for God.

Tom White, whose construction company built many Boston-area landmarks, including the Foxboro Stadium and much of the Boston subway system, was named "America's best philanthropist" by *Time* magazine.[14] White has given away most of his fortune to help poor and hungry people, and he and his wife have the goal of giving the rest away by the time they die. "Fortunately, I've never cared about expensive toys, yachts and things. . . . I prefer to spend my money to help people. I get pleasure out of that," he told some fellow Bread for the World donors.

Even most Republicans admire Jimmy Carter as one of the greatest former presidents because of the way he and his wife Rosalyn have invested their enormous prestige and talents to promote human rights and give opportunity to poor people. They volunteer at Habitat for Humanity sites. Through the Carter Center, they have helped resolve conflicts and monitor elections in a number of countries, done much to eradicate the river blindness scourge in Africa, and in other creative ways contributed significantly to agricultural development on that continent. Millions have benefited.

Janet and Carl Nelson (not their real names) are another remarkable couple. Janet inherited her father's estate. Carl became president of an investment banking company while still in his thirties. Janet became involved in an inner-city program working with children and served on a juvenile justice commission. She had become embittered by the racial and economic injustices she saw, but gave her life to Christ when she saw two streams—the gospel and justice—converge. Her bitterness vanished by viewing the struggle for justice in the light of hope rather than anger. They and their two children became active in the "Faith Alive" renewal movement, participating with this program in local churches around the country. The family visited a number of poor countries, including the various ministries of Mother Teresa's Missionaries of Charity in Calcutta. At a Bread for the World weekend retreat "it all came together," Janet said. "I had been linking concern and action, faith and finance, and Bread gave me a vision of how to do that more effectively through advocacy." Janet volunteered to be one of Bread for the World's congressional district coordinators and later a state coordinator, was elected to its board of directors, and chaired the board for several years.

Carl, meanwhile, had spent much time in Honduras working among the poor and then heading up a disaster relief program in Guatemala following an earthquake. He was persuaded to serve as interim president of a university, an interim that lasted ten years. Carl is still active in managing investments, but through the years has also excelled at raising funds from people of means for charitable causes. He prays for each person before a visit. "It puts you in a pastoral role," he says. Both Janet and Carl have given hugely of their time, energy, and substance for others. "The more

I give for the kingdom, the more I receive to give away," Carl observes. "It is impossible to outgive the Father." And Janet adds, "Before conversion you are like this [she closes each hand], but after conversion your hands are open to receive and give."

# TEN

# Living Simply So That Others May Simply Live

Albert Schweitzer was once asked why he traveled second class. "Because there is no third class," he reportedly replied.

For most of us, living on enough would mean living on less, even if "enough" is defined much more generously than basic needs. Fewer gadgets, fewer clothes, and an end to impulsive buying, for example. For some, it might mean a smaller car, fewer cars, or a less expensive house.

There are several arguments to be made in favor of scaling back. The first is that it is simply better for us. It can mean reduced stress, less rushing, fewer distractions, more time for friends and family, and a chance to refocus life on things that matter. A recent poll shows that despite overall trends in the opposite direction, from 1990 to 1996, almost 20 percent of adult Americans chose lifestyle changes that involved earning less; and of those who did, 85 percent expressed satisfaction with the changes.[1]

A second case to be made for simpler living is that it is kinder to God's creation. Walking more and driving less, or driving a more energy-efficient vehicle, for example, saves nonrenewable fuel and spares the atmosphere of particles that not only harm living things, but increase the hazards of global warming.

A third argument, and the one this chapter will focus on, is that living more simply may enable people who are barely surviving to live. Simpler living does that, however, only if you take steps to transfer resources to people whose lives are at risk. Eating less and spending less on food, for example, might be good for your health. It would be for most Americans. The amount Americans spend overeating and then dieting to deal with the consequences would be more than enough to wipe out world hunger. But cutting back isn't going to feed anyone unless, say, you contribute the amount saved to a food bank, a relief and development agency, or a group advocating for hungry people.

The foundation for all three reasons is love for God and love for neighbor. Simpler living should not be an end in itself. As the millennium turned, almost eight hundred million people were chronically undernourished—living constantly without enough food. This goes on despite the fact that for several decades the means to end hunger has been available. Shortage of individual and collective will enables it to persist. For this reason, we can no longer think about hunger as inevitable. It has become a scandal.

Hunger is a scandal because it is a moral outrage and a violation of human dignity. But it is also a scandal in the biblical sense of alienating people from God. Hunger causes despair and loss of hope for some, and Jesus has said in the starkest of words that neglect of the hungry marks a faithlessness that separates many well-fed people from God.

It is not hunger in itself that is offensive, but the fact that people *needlessly* go hungry and that they do so in part because of the indifference of believers. Just as helping the hungry is a work of love that can draw people to Christ, so our lack of concern can be a stumbling block. It endangers not only the faith of those who suffer, but makes skeptics of some who see what is happening and conclude that faith in Christ is not to be taken seriously. That makes it a scandal. Dietrich Bonhoeffer wrote:

> To allow the hungry man to remain hungry would be blasphemy against God and one's neighbor, for what is nearest to God is precisely the need of one's neighbor. It is for the love of Christ, which belongs as much to the hungry man as to myself, that I share my bread with him and share my dwelling with the homeless. If the hungry man does not attain to faith, then the guilt falls on those who refused him bread. To provide the hungry man with bread is to prepare the way for the coming of grace.[2]

The way we live matters. It matters to God and it matters to others whose lives are affected. The point is not that a simpler style of life would eliminate hunger and poverty (it would not), but that a life given to God becomes focused on what God wills. Because God desires love and justice for the poor, we must desire the same. Because a life given to material excess violates God and those who lack the barest necessities, surrendering that life to God and, by grace, living a new way in Christ, is also what God desires. For most of us that means, among other things, spending less time and money on ourselves and becoming far more generous to those who are impoverished. That would be at least one giant step toward addressing the scandal of hunger.

## Choices Have Consequences

The six-year-old boy taken to an emergency room following an accident was given a glass of milk. "How deep shall I drink?" he asked. He came from a very poor family in which something as precious as milk had to be shared with six brothers and sisters. Drinking too deeply would cheat others. So he asked, "How deep shall I drink?"[3] It is a question for us as well. How deep shall we drink from the glass of prosperity?

Peter Singer, professor of philosophy at Princeton University, describes a movie portrayal of a poor Brazilian woman, Dora, who pockets one thousand dollars by getting a nine-year-old boy to follow her to an address. After buying a prized TV, Dora learns that the boy's vital organs will be sold for transplantations, so she sets out to save his life. Singer comments that moviegoers in affluent countries would quickly condemn Dora if she had kept her TV and not rescued the boy. Yet, he says, the average U.S. family spends almost one-third of its income on things no more necessary to life and health than Dora's new TV. He asks, why is it any worse for Dora to sell a homeless child to organ peddlers than for an American to spend money on non-essentials when that money, given to organizations like UNICEF (United Nations' Children's Fund) or Oxfam America, could save children's lives? "I'm saying that you shouldn't buy that new car, take that cruise, redecorate the house or get that pricey new suit." The morally decent life, Singer maintains, puts the value of a child's life ahead of going to fancy restaurants.[4]

Singer's words are upsetting because they tell the truth. The late James P. Grant, director of UNICEF, calculated that every five hundred dollars spent on the child survival program saves a child's life. That does not count benefits such as preventing blindness, mental impairments, or other disabilities. A life for five hundred dollars. Considering that, does your desire for a new car or wide-screen television look any different?

Here is what relief and development organizations are telling me. The cost of a twenty-five-cent pack of gum can feed a refugee child for a day. The cost of a twenty-five-dollar shirt would buy fifty pounds of seed corn in Honduras, a month's care for an orphaned child, or school supply kits for two children in Africa. For the price of a modest television set, farmers in Peru can purchase several llamas, or a woman in India can buy an income-producing sewing machine. The cost of a five hundred–dollar appliance would give some family a heifer that would provide milk and income, or two water buffalo for plowing rice fields. A twenty-five hundred–dollar family vacation could build three adobe homes for hurricane victims in Central America.[5]

Now that I have spoiled your fun, let me add that God wants us to enjoy life, to have good times, and to spread the table well on special occasions. Jesus' attendance at a wedding feast at which he turned water into wine, his eating and drinking with sinners, and his acceptance of the woman's gift of costly ointment tell us something about this. But these things find their proper place only if we are opening our hearts with great generosity to others and not allowing personal gratification to rob them of opportunities for life and livelihood. Marva Dawn suggests saving favorite foods for the Sabbath or special celebrations and eating more simply the rest of the time. "One of the most important reasons for restoring a proper sense of feasting is so that we can be more responsible about caring for the hungry," she writes. "If we are gluttons all of the time, we do not know what it means to go without luxury, much less the essentials."[6]

Such sacrifices usually heighten rather than diminish our enjoyment of life. Family games, hikes, or outings yield more memorable pleasure than the commercialized, usually passive pastimes we have grown to depend on. We do well to ask, when considering a movie, a dinner out, or refurnishing the house, does this prepare me to give more of myself to others? Or would I simply drink deeply at their expense?

"You are not making a gift to the poor man from your possessions, but you are returning what is his. For what is common has been given for the use of all, you make exclusive use of it. The earth belongs to all, not to the rich," said St.

Ambrose. The first thing he did, upon being appointed bishop of Milan in the fourth century A.D., was to distribute his wealth to the poor—some directly, some indirectly through management of investments for the community.[7]

In his encyclical, *On the Development of the Peoples*, Pope Paul VI cites the above words of St. Ambrose, to emphasize "how seriously the Fathers of the Church described the obligation of the affluent to those in need."[8] During and beyond its early centuries, the church retained a strong sense of the goods of creation as meant for the good of all. This emphasis was often lost in Protestant circles. John Tropman notes that "the Catholic Ethic has a more communally oriented conception of the public good than the Protestant Ethic, which is more acquisitively oriented."[9] Acquisition, however, may be the culture of choice for Catholics as well as Protestants in America today. If so, both groups have neglected a cherished heritage.

The way of the cross involves sacrifice. We can rein in our spending and give willingly so that others might have reason to praise God for the gift of life. Far from denying us joy, however, such generosity brings far more satisfaction than does the pursuit of things for ourselves. Our fear of letting go—like a child who clutches a toy, crying "Mine! Mine!"—causes us to miss out on a freedom that God, who is in the business of producing cheerful givers, longs for us to have.

## Why Me, Lord?

"Why me? Why did God let this happen to me?" People say this—I have, and perhaps you have, too—when facing a major setback such as an accident, a disability, a divorce, a wayward child, a lost job, or a death in the family. But the question is one that we should be asking with regard to privileges rather than setbacks. I was born in the United States, a land of freedom and opportunity. I had two parents who loved and cared for me, who nourished my spirit even more

134

richly than my body. I went to good schools, never stood in an unemployment line, had a career that gave me more satisfaction than I could ever have imagined, had a cherished family, and by the standards of most of the world I am rich. Why me, Lord?

The answer is simple, for Jesus said, "from the one who has been entrusted with much, much more will be asked" (Luke 12:48). God has plans for us, and the more we have been given, the bigger the plans. You have been given much? Congratulations! God has great plans for you. But the plans call for giving, not getting; and serving, not being served.

That being the case, we need to think carefully about what we are doing for ourselves in relation to what we are doing for others. If, for example, we are among the average Americans using up an inordinate share of the earth's resources—drinking too deeply—is not God asking us to live simply and leave more for others? For most of us, being part of the world's 20 percent that receives more than 80 percent of its income, the answer is "Yes."

Be forewarned, however, that living more simply is not always simple. Even recycling paper, plastic, and bottles takes a bit of time and effort. So does saving energy. Years ago, I moved from Denver to New York with a car and soon sold it, because most of my work as a parish pastor and then as Bread for the World's executive was within walking distance and public transportation was readily available. When Bread for the World relocated to Washington, D.C., I continued without a car for about a year by biking several miles to work. That, along with distances for shopping and using public transportation proved time-consuming. My time was of far more value to hungry people than the dollars saved, so I bought a used car.

Some steps toward simplicity offer immediate rewards— like turning off the TV and reading or having a family evening. Other steps are harder. Helping aged parents is a cherished responsibility, but not always easy. Volunteering to tutor children, lead a youth group, or work in a soup kitchen takes time. Sharing the gospel with others takes effort. Prayer and reading the Bible take discipline. Generosity to people in need and for the mission of the church requires sacrifice. But even the more difficult steps will bring rewards if we serve faithfully and patiently.

The lines are never drawn the same for everyone. Many people around the world need to be able to create more wealth so they can obtain food, clothing, shelter, health care, and education. For most of them, washing clothes by hand makes sense (not that they have much choice)—but for most of us in industrialized countries, a washing machine is a great time-saver. We should not take that advantage for granted, however. The washer, too, should be used with thanksgiving, along with the awareness that most people in the world do not have anything so lavish, and that God is giving us this gift so it can be used in love and service. Perhaps the washer gives us more time to nurture our children in the way of Christ. Perhaps the time enables us to help a neighbor. Perhaps it allows us to earn money that could be contributed to an overseas mission or our church's relief and development agency.

Whatever advantage an appliance, a vacation, a remodeled house, or a raise in salary may give us, we need to ask, "Why me, Lord?" But then we should look to the Lord and not to a golden calf for the answer.

## A Couple of Complications

"A simple lifestyle takes more time, but it is more peaceful and helps us to be in touch with God," a friend writes—a good reminder that our goal is to become more fully the kind of people God would have us be. But it does take time and effort. Two complications deserve special attention.

The first is marriage and family. If you live alone, simplifying your life may not be easy, but it is relatively uncomplicated. Living with other people brings complications. For instance, one of the most common sources of conflict between married couples has to do with finances. Why? In part because two people are bound to have different needs and opinions. But it is also true that in our culture men more than women tend to establish an identity outside the home—hence decor and dust are of limited concern to most men. Women, on the other hand, tend to identify more with the home, so its furnishings usually mean more to them. Married couples need to make accommodations to that reality. Both men and women are tempted to achieve a sense of self that is attached to trappings; the trappings merely differ. Add children to this mix, and you have a trove of needs and demands to deal with. All of which underscores the importance of building on a common understanding of who we are in Christ and how we can help one another live faithfully instead of chasing mammon.

The responsibilities of marriage and family explain why Jesus and the apostle Paul encouraged consideration of celibacy as a calling for the sake of the kingdom. That possibility should be taken seriously today, not as a superior or inferior way of life, but as an opportunity for more undivided attention to a particular work of God. Some, who have the gift, may choose celibacy. For others, the single life may be chosen for them. Either way, it should be offered to God with thanksgiving, just as marriage and family life should be.

The second complication has to do with the matter of economic growth. When consumer spending drops and the economy fails to grow, unemployment and poverty increase. So how do we reconcile simplified living with the reliance of both poor and affluent people on consumer spending for their employment? The question, I believe, is largely academic. If personal spending is reduced to give to people in need, the recipients will spend the money. This will not depress the economy or reduce unemployment. If anything, it will shift spending to more basic needs. We can follow the urging of Jesus and the biblical witness confident that we are helping, not hurting people.

A growing economy is necessary (though not sufficient) for the creation of jobs that enable people to overcome hunger and poverty. But a growing economy is not necessarily a healthy economy. It may ravage the earth or enrich some at the expense of others. One way of multiplying the impact of simplified living is to work for responsible growth that protects the earth's resources for future generations and expands opportunities for everyone. In this way, too, we can help tame mammon.

## Linking Personal Efforts to Public Policy

Simplified living combined with generosity in giving can contribute importantly to our own lives, to the care of the earth, and to other people. In doing so, it can also sharpen our awareness of needs in all three areas. But simplified living is no panacea for the ills of nature and society. As a cure-all, it is like spooning water from a sinking ship. Link it with steps to seek public justice, however, and you have a powerful combination. A few illustrations show why.

Not throwing your family's picnic trash in the river is a public service, and it sends a message to the kids. But getting laws enacted and enforced that impose stiff penalties for the dumping of industrial and agricultural waste into that river might accomplish much more. We ought to do the former without neglecting the latter.

Herbert Hoover played an outstanding role, with government support and encouragement, in rescuing Europeans after World War I by mobilizing U.S. citizens to help send food, clothing, and medical supplies abroad. But when he became U.S. president and the Great Depression occurred, his heavy reliance on private efforts proved inadequate, and his presidency failed to meet the challenge. After World

War II, private assistance again played a key role in helping destitute Europeans; but to that assistance was added the government's Marshall Plan, which poured in billions of dollars to rebuild Europe's economy and prevent countries from turning to communism. Without the Marshall Plan, continued suffering in Europe would have led to a very different postwar history, to the detriment of us all.

Julius Nyerere, a devout Catholic, is revered as the father of Tanzania following the independence of its two predecessor states in the early 1960s. In contrast to almost all of Africa's postcolonial leaders—or national heads-of-state anywhere, anytime—Nyerere chose to live a simple, modest life, without the usual ornaments of privilege. Unfortunately, the socialist policies he pursued (understandable as a reaction to the capitalism imposed on Africa by European colonial powers) proved unworkable, and as a result Tanzania remained mired in poverty during and beyond the two decades of his presidency. Nyerere's personal life was exemplary in every way, but misguided policies undermined that legacy.

Think also about the conservation of fossil-fuel energy, which is of vital importance for several reasons. First, excessive use is costly and wasteful. The United States, with less than 5 percent of the world's population, uses about one-fourth of the world's energy. Second, fossil fuel pollutes the atmosphere. The United States contributes 25 percent of the world's greenhouse gases, again more than five times its share. Third, fossil-fuel energy is a nonrenewable resource that will eventually run out, but we act as though it will last forever. Fourth, two-thirds of the earth's proven oil reserves are in the Middle East, a politically volatile area. Our dependence upon its oil is risky both in terms of future supply and our ability to work for peace without the undue influence of losing that supply. For all of these reasons, it makes sense for us to adopt habits that use less commercial energy.

Although lifestyle changes to save energy have become fairly widespread, they have not, by themselves, proven to be very effective. When the oil-producing countries reduced the supply in the early 1970s, energy prices soared, the public was alarmed, and energy use dropped substantially for about a decade. Many voices in and out of government urged people to use energy more efficiently. People did. Cars and appliances were manufactured to use less fuel, and homes were installed with tighter windows and better insulation. When the price of energy dropped, so did fuel-efficient habits. In the United States, as household size kept shrinking, the size of new houses kept growing, and were stuffed with energy-hungry features such as central air-conditioning. Cars got bigger too. Despite improved technologies, energy use per person returned almost to its previous high levels. Price, far more than lifestyle considerations, fueled these changes.

A gradual increase in taxes on all nonrenewable energy would induce people to make energy-efficient decisions, as they did in the '70s and early '80s. Auto makers, for example, would soon build more fuel-efficient cars if consumer demand changed. Energy-efficiency standards, gradually strengthened, would have a similar effect. Raising the fuel efficiency of U.S. motor vehicles to forty miles per gallon would save more than the 1.7 million barrels of oil that the United States imports daily from Saudi Arabia.[10] Other steps in that direction would be to invest more public funds in the research and development of alternative sources of energy and to provide tax breaks for persons who switch to alternative energy. Moves such as these require policy action.

The message, then, is clear: personal steps to care for the earth, conserve resources, and assist others are necessary, but far from adequate. Combined with wise public policies, however, they are powerful agents of change.

140

# ELEVEN

# Love and Justice

As a child, Alice Gahana survived two concentration camps during the Holocaust. Asked what she remembered most, she replied, "The empty windows." German soldiers came to her little village when she was nine years old and told her family to come to the village square. "I walked that morning carrying my suitcase, down our cobble-stoned street—the street that I had walked all my life, by houses in which lived people I had known all my life. . . . But as I walked down the street, I noticed the windows were empty. No one came to the windows. My friends and neighbors knew what was happening, they knew—but they were afraid. Nobody came to the windows to see what was happening to me."[1]

Her story describes the failure of personal compassion; but that failure is tied immediately to a grave public injustice, an injustice that was able to flourish because millions of nominal Christians failed to demonstrate compassion. Lack of compassion and injustice are inseparable.

Jesus came to pour out God's love for the world. He also came to bring justice—not in addition to love, but as a part of love. This was clear at the outset of his public ministry, when at the synagogue in Nazareth he opened the scroll of the prophet Isaiah and read: "The Spirit of the Lord is on me because he has anointed me to preach good news to the poor. He has sent me to proclaim freedom for the prisoners and recovery of sight for the blind, to release the oppressed, to proclaim the year of the Lord's favor" (Luke 4:18–19). "The year of the Lord's favor" refers to the Year of Jubilee, when slaves were to be freed, debts forgiven, and land returned to the families who once owned it. Jesus' mission of love embraced not just personal generosity to the poor, but also justice.

A similar passage from Isaiah, used in the Gospel of Matthew, signals that the Lord's chosen servant "will proclaim justice to the nations" and work until "he leads justice to victory" (Matt. 12:18, 20). His justice, of course, was ultimately the justice of mercy, the Just One dying for the unjust to reconcile us to God. But his justice also extended to physical pain and economic oppression, as his constant reaching out to sick people, poor people, and social castoffs showed—much to the alarm of the authorities.

Jesus publicly challenged religious leaders who tithed spices, but neglected "justice and the love of God." "You should have practiced the latter," he said, "without leaving the former undone" (Luke 11:42). Jesus did not condemn their tithing small things, but he deplored their neglect of what matters most to God. To follow Jesus, then, means to pursue a love that includes justice.

142

## Justice as a Form of Love

When one family goes hungry, we offer food or the means to obtain it. That is the way of love. But what if one family becomes thousands or millions of families? Personal charity is no longer adequate. A much larger corporate response becomes necessary.

Suppose that in the course of helping one family, you learn that they lack food because of medical emergencies and that the parent's job does not include health insurance for the family. Or that the father, who has limited skills, is working in exchange for public assistance; but with the time limit for such assistance about to run out and with unemployment rising, he has poor prospects for getting a decent-paying job. You may still offer food, but the long-term help needed for this family and for countless others in comparable situations may require policy decisions that will enable them to get health care or obtain decent employment. In that case, love means working with others to bring about changes so that families can live responsibly without going hungry. In other words, love requires justice.

When I was a boy, my father used to say, "It's better to build a fence at the top of the cliff than to have an ambulance at the bottom." I thought of that often as a pastor on the Lower East Side of New York, because I found myself constantly dealing with emergencies—driving the ambulance. So I attempted to build a fence by helping to start Bread for the World as a citizens' movement against hunger.

We *are* our brother's and sister's keeper, and the ethic of love compels us to engage in personal charity. Without personal charity, society has no heart. As essential as it is, however, personal charity falls woefully short of addressing many needs in a society as large and complex as our own. That is true even when private charity is organized on a large scale, because it is inevitably limited in scope and

143

spotty in coverage. The two wealthiest city council districts in Manhattan, for example, have more soup kitchens than the two poorest districts because of where the donors, not the hungry people, are concentrated.[2] So love calls for justice as well as charity. Private charity and public justice are like two legs. The solution to hunger and many other social ills requires the use of both.

The Hebrews, guided by Moses and the prophets, understood this. There is no sharp distinction in the Old Testament between justice and charity, for obedience included both personal and corporate obligations. That the Jubilee was proclaimed on the Day of Atonement underscores this inseparable link.

Land was capital, the primary means of livelihood. The Hebrew understanding of land ownership and distribution was one way (among several) of securing legislative justice for the poor rather than making them depend on the uncertain impulses of others. Charity, however, especially toward aliens, the fatherless, and widows, was also clearly mandated. In this way, personal kindness and corporate justice were inextricably linked. What the Lord requires of us, said the prophet Micah, is to act justly, show mercy, and walk humbly with God (Micah 6:8). Justice and kindness were essential aspects of the peace, or *shalom*—the well-being and wholeness of a right relationship with God and one another—that God wished for people individually and collectively.

The intent was that the people as a whole prospered or suffered together, and they were told that God's blessing was related to their treatment of those without independent means of survival (Deut. 14:28–29). Today that may mean such things as policies to ensure that everyone has basic health care and enough to eat.

Seeing poverty as injustice, the prophets were aroused. They unnerved the well-to-do by announcing God's judgment against them for trampling the poor, even selling innocent people for a pair of shoes (Amos 2:6). Because they

144

oppressed the poor, the Lord despised their religious assemblies, their songs, and their sacrifices. Instead, said Amos, "let justice roll on like a river, righteousness like a never-failing stream!" (5:24 NIV).

Jesus identified with this prophetic tradition. He condemned attachment to wealth and cared openly for the poor and for other social and religious rejects. He rebuked the rich not because they were rich or because they were violating the letter of the law, but because of their blindness to the needs of others. And he blessed the poor not because of their poverty, but because they had been told by religious authorities that they were worth little or nothing in the eyes of God; yet in their poverty they more readily humbled themselves before God and more eagerly received the good news of the kingdom.

The "righteousness" for which Jesus urged us to hunger and thirst (Matt. 5:6) can also be translated "justice." We are to hunger and thirst for the goodness of God that embraces both.

To follow Jesus is to offer all of life to the one who gave his life for us. Consequently, ours is a high commitment to love and justice. We cannot, however, expect a secularized *nation* to operate on the basis of that commitment. But as part of our commitment to Jesus, we can ask the nation for a reasonable measure of public justice, for which it is accountable to God. The offering of ourselves to Christ should include the thought and effort to weigh in as citizens so that the best possible expression of justice is achieved. To do so is the way of love.

Most readers of this book live in a democracy, a government of the people. To paraphrase Pogo, an old cartoon character, we have met "the powers that be" and they are us. This extraordinary gift from God gives us a holy obligation to work for justice. Such work is always a struggle, always flawed. But struggle we must for the sake of the poorest and weakest among us, and for the good of everyone else.

Not to work for such justice is loveless. It is to be complicit in the greed of socially ingrained arrangements that favor the "haves" over the "have nots," the powerful at the expense of the weak.

In 1630, John Winthrop, governor of the Massachusetts Bay Colony, preached a sermon, "Christian Charity: A Model Hereof," to his fellow immigrants while still aboard the ship *Arbella*. He spoke of the seductions of self-interest and ambition as no less dangerous to the common good than famine and pestilence, which were to kill many. "There are two rules whereby we are to walk one towards another: justice and mercy," he said, proposing "more enlargement [of heart] toward others and less respect toward ourselves."[3] By that standard, the record of U.S. Christians and of the nation is mixed, with some landmarks of great justice, others of great violation and neglect. Injustices continue to rob many of dignity and life, and for that reason love compels us to seek justice.

"Out of the crooked timber of humanity no straight thing was ever made," said the philosopher Immanuel Kant.[4] That fact underscores the inevitable imperfection of justice, as well as the need to work diligently for it.

## More Than Private Piety

We are prone to think of our response to God purely in terms of personal behavior and private assistance. Essential as these are, they still fall short without public justice. What use is it to live a simplified life, volunteer at a food bank, and contribute money, while doing nothing about public policies that lock people deeply into hunger? Is it sinful to waste money but okay to waste influence that could bring a far greater benefit to the poor?

Government was instituted by God with responsibility to pursue public justice. Citizens, in turn, have a responsibility to guide public officials toward that purpose. For example, private food assistance helps millions of people in the U.S., but the government's food stamp program is many times larger, and its coverage, though inadequate, is far more complete. Similarly, private aid helps countless poor people abroad. But the U.S. government commands more resources and its action sways decisions of other donor countries as well as international aid agencies. In addition, only the government can determine policies in areas such as trade, taxation, and foreign affairs—areas that directly affect poor people. So unless people of compassion reach lawmakers with their concerns for justice, the poor are certain to be oppressed and those who are prosperous are sure to obtain favorable treatment at their expense.

For many, God is the God of our personal life, but not of economics and government, which supposedly isn't God's turf. That puts much of life off-limits to God and denies the truth that Jesus Christ is the Lord of a believer's whole life, not just selected parts of it. Christians often behave like believers when it comes to private morality, but not when it comes to public justice. They are then far more apt to judge economic and political policies by how their pocketbooks are affected, not by how these policies affect others. All of this plays squarely into the hands of the culture of mammon, which, having reduced faith to private life, claims everything else. Privatized faith becomes our "tithe"—the part of life that God gets. In this way, our lives become shaped by secular values rather than those of Christ.

That would be bad enough if it did injury only to ourselves. Unfortunately, it harms others as well. When Hitler rose to power in Germany, the church for the most part played it safe. Universities and other institutions were even more compliant, to be sure, and there were many courageous exceptions among Christians and Christian leaders; but the usual stance was, "Let the church preach the gospel and stay out of politics." We now know the folly of such quietism. Far from being "out of politics," the church was deeply involved, because silence was seen as consent. Partly as a result of this silence, the Nazis unleashed bloodshed and genocide that destroyed millions of lives.

But what is the difference between that silence and being part of a nation with unprecedented wealth that ignores millions of impoverished people dying needlessly every year from hunger and disease? There is a difference, of course. In one case, evil intent drives the killing. In the other, it is largely a matter of neglect. But Jesus did not say, in his description of the great judgment, "You killed the hungry, you cheated the naked, you assaulted the poor." He said, in effect, "When I was hungry, thirsty, naked, imprisoned—when I was desperate for your help—you ignored me. You passed by on the other side." Neglect.

In some important ways, the United States does respond to the world's poor. It encourages democracy and human rights, and for all of its flaws, the U.S. economy does help lift the economy of many other countries. Thousands of private charitable organizations, supported by millions of donors, assist needy people everywhere. When famine threatens, U.S. food assistance plays a leading role. None of these things should be forgotten. But there is also the matter of proportion. What are we, as a nation, doing with what we have? Considering what we have and the desperate need of others, we do pathetically little.

The average annual income per person (including dependents) in the United States is about thirty thousand dollars as I write. The poorest 1.2 billion people worldwide live on less than one dollar per person a day. The United States spends about forty-five hundred dollars per person each year on health care. The average spent on health care per person in the world's sixty poorest countries—thirteen dollars.

Although the United States has a nine trillion dollar annual economy, it ranks *last* among twenty-one donor nations when its official assistance to poor countries is measured as a percentage of income. Only one-tenth of 1 percent of its annual national income (and one-half of 1 percent of the federal budget) is designated for food and development aid to poor countries.

If a nine trillion dollar economy grows by 3 percent in a given year, the *increase alone* amounts to $270 billion. What could the richest nation in the history of the world do if it decided to share a more significant part of that increase with poor people? According to the British chancellor of the exchequer, Gordon Brown, $50 billion a year in additional development aid by wealthier countries could, within fifteen years, cut world poverty in half, cut child mortality by two-thirds, and guarantee a primary education for every child.[5] The U.S. share (one-fourth of that additional aid) would cost $13 billion a year—less than six percent of the $270 billion increase in U.S. income, or thirteen cents a person per day. Along the same lines, economist Jeffrey Sachs writes:

> The rich countries are so rich and the poor so poor that a few added tenths of one percent of GNP from the rich ones ramped up over the coming decades could do what was never before possible in human history: Ensure that the basic needs of health and education are met for all impoverished children in this world.[6]

Bread for the World estimates that ending hunger in the United States and paying its share for cutting world hunger in half within fifteen years might cost an additional seven cents a day per American. This rough estimate indicates that dramatic progress against hunger is readily affordable. *That we fail to do what we can to reduce hunger is a scandal that lies at the feet of U.S. Christians who could easily insist that the nation rise to this challenge.* To place the need next to our affluence, and then to consider the call of Jesus, is to weep—weep for the poor, and weep for ourselves. The words of

Thomas Jefferson may fit us as well as they fit a generation that (including Jefferson) tolerated slavery: "I tremble for the nation, when I reflect that God is just."

Your eyes may glaze over the statistics. But see for a moment a scene in an East African refugee camp, where a visitor is surrounded by young children and notices that one of them has a badly infected eye with insects crawling on it. "Would someone help this boy?" he asks. The camp director replies sadly, "We can only take care of emergencies."[7]

## Making a Difference

What I am suggesting as a responsible bare minimum for the United States and other high-income countries is hardly a sacrifice, but merely the sharing of a small fraction of their income growth with the world's poor. It would be a modest contribution for us, but would make a huge difference for them. For example, an additional twenty-six dollars a year in health care for someone in the United States brings only a marginal benefit; but it would *triple* health care spending in the poorest sixty countries, making possible the saving of countless lives through preventive measures and enabling people to work more productively. Similar gains would apply to targeted assistance for nutrition, food production, education, and micro-credit for starting up small enterprises, to cite other examples.

The kind of assistance I speak of would not simply save lives, but help people work their way out of hunger and poverty. Joe Short, former head of Oxfam America, tells about watching food arrive in Cambodia during a time of famine. People clapped politely in appreciation. Then some fishing nets were unloaded and the people cheered! The food might sustain them for a few weeks, but the fishing nets enabled them to sustain themselves indefinitely.

In the long run, U.S. generosity would return dividends in the form of a more secure world, less conflict, and even stronger economies for donor nations. The Marshall Plan for European recovery and the G.I. Bill to send veterans to college, for example, each brought immense economic dividends, even though that was not in the mind of most Americans who simply thought they were doing the right thing. The same would almost certainly be true today, if a commitment were made to reduce hunger and poverty.

As citizens, we have a share of responsibility for the nation's wealth as well as our own, and we must do our part to see that it serves at least a minimal justice for those struggling to survive. Here, too, it is clear that we are far from helpless—though most of us seem to believe that we are. On the contrary, we can make a telling intervention for others. I have seen it again and again each year at Bread for the World, as thousands of ordinary citizens write letters and contact members of Congress on a few key issues. Their efforts have leveraged benefits to hungry people in dollar value alone of a hundred times or more the amount contributed, not to count the far more important benefit of lives saved, suffering lessened, and opportunities opened. What Bread for the World and others have not been able to do so far, however, is obtain that critical mass of support necessary to bring about a national commitment to end hunger in the United States and eventually end most hunger worldwide. But it can and should be done.

The Jubilee 2000 campaign showed how that might happen. In 1990, Martin Dent, a British political scientist, and a handful of his students (some from developing countries) were deeply moved by the witness of Africans regarding the burden of their countries' international debts. Those debts resulted in millions of children being unable to attend school, and health care services reduced to almost nothing. Poor countries around the world had borrowed heavily during the 1970s and early 1980s because oil-producing countries had forced prices skyward. Rich countries encouraged poor countries to borrow money to buy fuel to keep their economies going. Then interest rates soared, and poor countries with stagnant economies found themselves unable to repay their loans; even the attempt to do so dried up funds for health care, education, and other development needs. Debtor nations seemed chained to perpetual poverty, to raising illiterate children and seeing many of them die.

Martin Dent latched onto the idea of the Old Testament Jubilee, which included forgiveness of debts every fiftieth year. The idea started to catch on, primarily in Christian circles, and soon organizations around the world began supporting it. Before long, Pope John Paul II, Archbishop Desmond Tutu, U.S. Catholic bishops, and other religious leaders endorsed the campaign, as did various church bodies. Country by country, church-led coalitions formed that included charitable agencies, businesses, unions, and other organizations. The media began to take notice.

In the United States, Bread for the World worked with Oxfam and church representatives to draft a bill and get it introduced in Congress. The bill proposed debt forgiveness for the poorest countries, with conditions to ensure its use for initiatives to reduce poverty. Bread members and others sent about two hundred thousand letters to Capitol Hill and visited members of Congress. One result was that a small number of key congressional conservatives began to champion the bill. That got the attention of the White House, and soon the Clinton administration began urging its adoption. In the end, Congress enacted legislation that wrote off an initial $435 million of debt, paving the way for further debt relief in subsequent years. Each U.S. dollar leverages about twenty additional dollars in debt relief from other countries, the World Bank, and the International Monetary Fund.

This campaign demonstrated the kind of initiative that could reduce much of the world's hunger and poverty. For that to happen, however, many more Christians will have to put their citizenship in service to Christ. Can we hear God's wake-up call for the taming of mammon and begin to advocate justice? That, too, is part of love and a way of following Christ.

# Saying "Yes" to Life

In *The Cost of Discipleship*, Dietrich Bonhoeffer reminds us that when Christ calls us, he bids us come and die.[1] So he does. But the greater truth is that in doing so, he bids us come and live.

"Follow me," Jesus said. The disciples followed, because it was an invitation to live. They learned along the way that taking up the cross was part of the package, that receiving life also included the relinquishing of life. Yet we have no record of the disciples complaining about what they had left behind to follow Jesus, because the gift of the kingdom is so stunningly good that what they gave up pales by comparison.

When Jesus says, "Follow me," our instinct may be to ask, "What must we give up?" But this response is like saying, "Tell us, so we will know what we can keep for ourselves." That allows us to play both sides of the street. It reveals an attachment to mammon and to the gods of the world—the very things from which Jesus would rescue us.

The first question, then, is not, "What must we give up?" but, "What do we receive?" For if we receive from Jesus a new life with God that begins now and never ends, then the giving of life to God is more joy than sacrifice.

"What must we give up?" is not the second question, either. The second question is, "What can I do *with* the life God has given me?"

Ansgar Sovik illustrates what I mean. Sovik has had a long and distinguished career as professor of religion and Asian history at St. Olaf College, where he also helped launch and guide an international studies program that sends two-thirds of St. Olaf students abroad for part of their studies. In retirement, one of his activities was to make bookends from the timber of old buildings being renovated at St. Olaf and give the bookends away before Christmas to anyone who agreed to contribute twenty-five dollars to world relief or advocacy against hunger. Over the years, he has sent thousands of dollars to Bread for the World from this activity alone. When I expressed amazement at what he had done with his (then) eighty-five years, Sovik told me how blessed he has been from childhood on. He said that from the time he was a young boy, his father always greeted him (in Norwegian) with the words, "Are you saying 'yes' to life, my son?"

That greeting is a treasure. Are we saying "yes" to life? yes to the Lord of life? to the world that God created and sent his Son to save? to our gifts? to the needs and opportunities that surround us? to the cries of the poor?

That, it seems to me, is the response Jesus is seeking. The emphasis ought clearly to be on the good that God calls us to do: in our daily work, nurture of family, deeds of mercy, peace, justice, the sharing of the gospel, the nourishing of the soul, the care of the earth. Doing such things is our purpose. Jesus' invitation to give possessions to the poor, for example, has to be seen as part of this "yes," a chance to accomplish great good with our lives, part of the joy set before us that enables us to take up the cross and follow him.

Saying "yes" to life embraces all things. It includes seeing the miracle of creation through the eyes of a child. More than that it means seeing everything, however imperfectly, through the eyes of God—seeing the world and all that is in it the way God sees it and the way God wills it to be, and discovering that in doing so, it becomes a truly new creation. It means looking at others and relating to others through the heart and the mind of Christ. If we practice this, not giving up when we stumble, but returning to it because it is the truth, then letting go of what God wants us to give up becomes much easier. It is a "yes" rather than a "no" to life.

To focus on what we have to give up makes the Christian life a burdensome undertaking, one that invites non-compliance, grudging compliance, or legalistic compliance. In each case, it shifts the attention to the self. But the self is precisely what Jesus says we have to lose if we want to find life through him.

Focusing primarily on things we should give up or things we cannot do gives us a pinched outlook and turns us inward on our always abundant shortcomings. Worse yet, it gives us amnesia regarding things we ought to do, surely one of Satan's more clever tricks, causing us to lose sight of opportunities for speaking the gospel and responding to needs that surround us. God's purpose for us is not simply that we empty ourselves of vices, but that we fill ourselves with the goodness of Christ. Otherwise, we miss the warning of Jesus, who said that when an unclean spirit leaves someone and returns to find that person empty, it brings seven other spirits more evil than itself to move in again (Matt. 12:43–45).

The renunciation of possessions, which Jesus asks of us, is not a rejection of the world, but an invitation to say "yes" to the world. When I was a seminary intern, I heard D. T. Niles, a well-known evangelist from India, preach on John 3:16. He said that Christians are twice-converted people.

They are converted first from the world to Jesus Christ. Then, he said, they are converted again to the world, but not as before. This time it is to love the world through the heart and mind of Christ.

The woman who broke social convention and poured a flask of expensive ointment on Jesus just days before his cru-cifixion—this woman, who seemed aware, as his disciples were not, of what awaited him in Jerusalem—knew how to say "yes" to Jesus and to life. She displayed the same kind of abandon that enabled Jesus to possess nothing, yet to enjoy feasts and friendship immensely.

I thought of that woman a few days ago when making a quick visit to the hospital. Parked in front was a pickup truck full of stuffed animals for sale, intended presumably for sick or injured children. A bundled-up woman stood by, look-ing for buyers. "Consumer culture," I noted mentally. Then the thought ran through my mind, "I bet she has a hard time earning enough to support her family; and probably so do the factory workers who make those things." And it occurred to me that buying a stuffed animal for a child in need of love could also be a way of saying "yes" to life.

### God's "Yes" to Us

Our saying "yes" to life is based upon God's "yes" to us. Without that, we would not be free to say "yes" to God. That may sound too obvious to mention, but in fact we do not instinctively hear God's "yes." Our churches are full of peo-ple who deep within feel that God is the God of "no." He is the God who restricts our behavior, forbids us to do things, says "Thou shalt not," and is waiting to zap us if we step over the line. "Everything I want to do is either sinful or fatten-ing," a teenager complained.

Gerard Straub describes giving money to an elderly, homeless woman who was panhandling near upscale Toluca Lake, California. She was surprisingly lucid, but unwilling to say anything about herself except her name, Dolores. Because her clothes looked filthy and the weather was cold, Straub and his wife brought her a small bundle of warm, clean clothes. These she rejected. Straub reflects:

> In terms of riches, I am to God what Dolores is to me. . . . God wants to give me everything I need. And I tell God I don't need anything, I can handle it myself.
>
> Slowly, I am waking up to the fact that I need God for absolutely everything, and that without God I am just a lonely, cold man living on a corner near God's infinitely bountiful kingdom.[2]

We simply do not fathom God's great "yes" to us.

That "yes" was evident when God pronounced the creation "very good." We humans were created in God's image, to reflect what God is like in ways that no other earthly creature can—another "yes." But we are fallen creatures, and that good image has become badly tarnished. True. But God also set out to restore creation and, through Jesus, to restore us as well. That is the great drama that unfolds in the Bible, which brings us the news that all of God's promises find their "yes" in Christ (2 Cor. 1:20). It gets even better. "How great is the love the Father has lavished on us, that we should be called children of God!" (1 John 3:1).

Even "thou shalt nots" reflect God's "yes" to us. Check Exodus 20. The commandments begin not with, "You shall have no other gods before me," but, "I am the Lord your God, who brought you out of Egypt, out of the land of slavery." Look what I have done for you! God says. Therefore, have no other gods. The prohibitions that follow also reflect God's love, for they serve as a guardrail to prevent us from falling into the sea. For example, God created us as sexual beings ("very good," he observes), so God is saying "yes" to sexual intimacy, not "no"—"yes" to the pleasure, the companionship, the intimate lifelong union and family with which God wishes to bless us. For that reason, God wants us to preserve this great expression of love for the marriage relationship for which it is intended. So even God's "no" to us is a "yes." For if God would withhold something from us, how could it possibly be good for us? And if God wants something for us, how can it possibly be bad?

All of us have difficulty hearing God's "yes" because it is so counter to our instincts, too good to be true, and we are so reluctant to trust that it is so. But the "yes" is there for us to build on. "All things are yours," Paul said (1 Cor. 3:21), whether the world, life or death, present or future. God isn't holding anything back. These are ours, and we belong to Christ. St. Augustine understood this well when he said, "Love God and do as you please," knowing that if we love God, pleasing God is what will please us. But then the psalmist thought of it first: "Delight yourself in the LORD and he will give you the desires of your heart" (37:4 NIV). Precisely!

## The Life of Compassion

A heart captivated by God's love is what God desires above all, because it is a heart that delights God, a heart that God can use, a heart that is free to love and serve. But a heart burdened by guilt, one that constantly strains to become worthy of God, is a paralyzed heart. A heart that treats forgiveness and acceptance by God as a cheap license for doing what it pleases is self-deceived. But God's forgiveness, received in faith, liberates the heart. Doing good for the God who has loved us in Christ becomes its consuming purpose, its joy; as a result, everything else begins to find its proper place. In just this way, God's "yes" to us is intertwined with our response, God's "yes" and ours joining in a symphony of love.

Let me illustrate. When David Beckmann left his shining career at the World Bank to head Bread for the World,

he told me that the two-thirds cut in salary was "pretty dras-
tic" for his family. They had to make adjustments and work
out differences of opinion about what kind of house to have.
Then a change in the Bank's retirement rules made compromise within the family easier, and Beckmann says, "It
seemed that God was pouring out blessings on us, as if to
say, 'Okay, stop worrying about money and get on with the
job.'" He adds, "At this point, the main obligation I feel is
to use my life energies toward the purposes God has given
me—primarily Bread for the World's mission and my family. My time is more valuable than our possessions, so my
first stewardship concern is to use my time well. In the end
I rest in God's grace. Despite my lack of austerity and sacrifice, God forgives and uses me."[3]

Beckmann's willingness to say "yes" to God and to life, at
no inconsiderable cost to himself and his family, has brought
benefits to millions of hungry people. It has also led to an
impressive celebration of grace.

We respond to God's "yes" with a special regard for
those in our most intimate orbit of responsibility and
those most deeply in need, using the gifts God has given
us in the special circumstances that each of us faces.
Because it is prompted by God and used by God, our
response (flawed though it is certain to be) is instrumen-
tal in transforming lives and influencing the culture. It
does so by the power of the gospel, the power of the cross
and resurrection, the power of the Holy Spirit. It stems
from a love that gives to human hearts and minds the
heart and mind of Christ.

Each of us says "yes" to someone or something. Ultimately,
there is no neutrality. We may say "yes" to God, or "yes" to
a god of our own or the world's fashioning; but as surely as
nature abhors a vacuum, before someone or something we
will bow. Each bow is an attempt to say "yes" to life; but if
the object of our desire is incapable of addressing the two
most fundamental human dilemmas—sin and death—we

are sure to come up short and invest ourselves in the culture of both. If we were made for communion with God, then is it not folly to pursue any other? Is it not folly if doing so violates our very being and the purpose for which we were made? To say "yes" to God, then, is to say "yes" to life—the life that God alone can give.

# THIRTEEN

# Filling the Heart with Something Better than Cash

Dear Lord, give bread to the hungry,
And hunger of Thee to those who have bread.

—ANONYMOUS

The human heart will be filled. If God is not the primary occupant, someone or something else will be. We speak of an emptiness of the heart, of course, but we mean by that a heart filled with things that do not satisfy, like empty calories that fill the stomach but fail to nourish the body. The culture of mammon has no shortage of clamoring tenants knocking at our heart's door. If we open our heart to them, we will be pushed and pulled by forces that quickly take control.

163

To live as children of God and not as cultural clones, we need to nourish the heart with the presence of God. One book series offers chicken soup for the soul, a modest step in the right direction. But more solid nourishment is essential. Against the attractions and anxieties that swirl about us, Jesus tells us to seek first the kingdom and righteousness of God (Matt. 6:33). That means allowing God to inform our lives through the witness of Moses and the prophets, Jesus and the apostles, and saints through the ages. In this way God becomes the center of everything.

The wisdom of Ecclesiastes teaches us that making ourselves the fixed point from which to view reality is a recipe for despair.[1] That touches a sensitive nerve today in a culture increasingly convinced that each individual is the source of what is right, wrong, and true. The result is often a do-it-yourself spirituality that tends to focus on personal fulfillment. How different from Jesus. He assumes that the fixed point is God the Father, who reveals wisdom to those who are as receptive as children rather than to those regarded as wise and learned (Matt. 11:25).

Robert Maynard, the first African American editor and publisher of a major U.S. metropolitan daily newspaper, *The Oakland Tribune*, discovered this the hard way. A high school dropout from the troubled Bedford-Stuyvesant section of Brooklyn, Maynard became a newspaper reporter and won a prized Neiman Fellowship at Harvard University at age twenty-nine. "I assumed that Harvard, a great institution founded by Congregational ministers, surely would help me understand how intellect should play a role in achieving social justice," he said. "Instead I got there and found myself confronting more bigotry than I had ever expected to find in a place of enlightenment. For years I was puzzled by that experience." For years he had also abandoned the church. Then he heard a sermon by Will Herzfeld. Speaking about the Pharisees, Dr. Herzfeld said they were "steeped in the light of learning, yet resisted the source of the light." A light flashed in Maynard's own mind. "That's it!" he said. "That's Harvard!" He framed the sentence that hung on the wall of his office until he died: "They are steeped in the light of learning, but they resist the source of the light."[2]

The psalmist reflected the same insight centuries before Christ: "In your light we see light," he wrote (Ps. 36:9 NIV).

## Prayer and Solitude

The heart will be filled. That is why Jesus asks us to hunger and thirst for the goodness of God. Doing so does not come naturally to us. On the contrary, it is natural for us to follow our own desires. So we begin always by inviting God to enter a heart that is instinctively unreceptive.

It should not surprise us, then, that prayer and time alone with God seem strange and out of place in a life that is occupied with many interests and responsibilities that make little allowance for anything so impractical. However, if the heart is to be properly filled, it must be emptied of things that leave no space for God, and give God access. Doing so means setting aside time for prayer and reflection. An empty prayer life reflects an emptiness in life, which is to say a cluttered and distracted heart.

Silence helps to sweep away the clutter and distractions. That can be frightening when we are so accustomed to constant sound—frightening precisely because the distractions allow us to avoid facing our true selves, alone with God. Yet in that silence, God allows us to begin a quiet conversation, listening as well as speaking, unburdening ourselves, and placing our entire lives at God's bidding.

We were made for communion with God, and prayer by definition is a confession that without God we are shorn of contentment. But it is God, not contentment, that we seek in prayer. To pray for the purpose of achieving contentment is to manipulate God, to make God a servant in giving us what we want. This is the opposite of prayer, because the object of prayer is to subject ourselves to God. "Be my God and let me be your servant," is the stance that prayer must take. Contentment usually follows, but it is never guaranteed; God may withhold it for a time to test and strengthen us so that we commit ourselves more fully to him, not our own happiness, in prayer.

There is much for which to pray, but we can start small. We do not need to imagine ourselves seasoned contemplatives. Persistence is essential, however, for if we pray only when we feel like it, we will pray hardly at all. Not feeling like praying is simply evidence that we need to do so.

We can be our true unpolished selves in God's presence, for even the apostle Paul counted on the Holy Spirit to make up for human weakness in prayer and intercede for him, translating those sighs that words cannot express (Rom. 8:26).

I long understood that the Lord's Prayer is a model, but only when going through the pain of an unwanted divorce did I become deeply attached to it as a guide for placing my life before God and calling upon God for help. The prayer is a model not as a ten-second recitation, but as a framework for approaching God as beloved children, for seeking God's will, for trust regarding all that we need and daily receive, for confessing sins and forgiving others, for help in time of trial and in the face of evil.

In our moments with God, we bring personal needs, opening our lives more fully to God, and in doing so allowing God access to our hearts. We need also to care for others in our prayers. Family members, friends, or neighbors may be troubled, perhaps having wandered from the path of life or experiencing grief or pain. Others, known or unknown to us, may be hungry, homeless, imprisoned, victims of violence. "If we genuinely love people, we desire for them far more than it is within our power to give, and that will cause us to pray," writes Richard Foster.[3]

"When our prayers are in order, everything else follows," David Beckmann once told me when I asked, "What is the single most important thing we can do about hunger?" One answer to prayer is that God helps us put our hearts and minds on things that matter. Action follows.

Social activists who are too busy changing the world to pray have special need of prayer, otherwise they are easily blinded by their own opinions. God tames our pride, gives us perspective, and helps us endure discouragement that might otherwise induce burnout. Early in life, Gary Arndt, a United Church of Christ pastor, felt called to overturn the wrongs of the world but discovered anger and frustration within himself over the lack of response. He was a man of peace with little inner peace. He decided that the mantra, "Do something, don't just pray!" wasn't working, so he began to pray and came to realize that he had been taking charge for God rather than serving on God's terms. Before long, he was chairing a spiritual development network of the UCC to foster contemplative social action.[4]

Jean Vanier, founder of l'Arche, an international movement providing homes for the mentally impaired, was the son of George P. Vanier, governor-general of Canada. Both were men of prayer. The son found beside his father's deathbed a book with these sentences heavily underlined:

> There is no use arguing about it, you are going to be asked to give daily to the combination of these three exercises: prayer, reflection and spiritual reading. No matter how busy you are, no man is too busy to eat; neither is any man too busy to feed his soul. And if we starve our souls, we will deprive our lives, busy though they may be, of their fruitfulness.[5]

Edward Skillin, longtime editor and publisher of *Commonweal,* an independent Roman Catholic magazine, was a man of unusual compassion who helped behind the scenes in the launching of Bread for the World. He affiliated, as a layman, with the Benedictine order, attempting to combine prayer and work, prayer and life. Among the things said about him at his funeral mass was the following:

> Close your eyes and listen to these lines from the great Rule of Saint Benedict: *O Lord, I place myself in your hands and dedicate myself to you. I pledge myself to do your will in all things—to love the Lord God with all my heart, all my soul, all my strength . . . Not to seek after pleasures . . . To relieve the poor. To clothe the naked. To visit the sick. To bury the dead. To help in trouble. To hold myself aloof from worldly ways . . . To speak the truth with heart and tongue . . . Not to be slothful. Not to be a murmurer. Not to be a detractor. To put my trust in God. . . .* You get the idea. This was Edward, living the Gospel, day by day. . . . At Edward's burial on Thursday, his daughter Susan recalled going as a child with her father to the *Commonweal* office. Outside the door there was a line of people, all in need of a handout, waiting to see 'Mr. Skillin.' He knew them all, many by name.[6]

Prayer and work, prayer and life, a heart in which God dwells—for this we were made and to this Jesus calls us.

## Praise and Thanksgiving

We do well to begin our days with prayer and our prayers with praise. Doing so puts everything in a different light. When God's love and majesty, God's glory shown in creation and redemption, and God's goodness to us and to others are lifted up in thanksgiving, other things fall into place. Possessions lose their luster. Problems don't seem so big. We find that in giving thanks we receive the gift of gratitude. Thanks to God for his goodness, for the gift of Jesus and our life in him, is the key to joy.

Ann Davis, an African American on the staff of Bread for the World years ago, led prayers one morning. Drawing on her own experience in a Pentecostal church, and with beaming face, she said, "We don't give enough praise here! We are always telling God about this problem and that problem, and asking for help; but we need to thank God for being so wonderful, for all of his blessings, and for sending his Son, Jesus, to save us!" She proceeded to offer a spontaneous prayer of joy and thanksgiving that palpably changed the atmosphere and taught all of us.

There is so much for which to praise God, so much that each of us has for which to be thankful. If it is right to thank someone who does us a small favor, surely the majesty and love of God, and God's awesome sacrifice to bring us into the kingdom, should make us eager beyond description to sing and shout with praise. More than noise is called for, of course. We can show deep emotion with exuberance or with quiet dignity, in Gregorian chant or gospel songs. Whatever the form, let it be a genuine, heartfelt, and beautiful expression of thanks—our best. If the coming of Christ causes heaven and nature to sing, is there any reason why any of us should be a tepid exception?

Praise may be hidden and unobserved in the most available places. The Lord's Prayer, for example, seems strangely devoid of thanksgiving and people have often wondered why. In reality, the entire prayer can be seen as praise to God. If we wish God's holy name to be honored, should we not be lifting up that name in the highest praise? And when we ask for daily bread, are we not expressing an immense gratitude to God for supplying every need of body and life? And on it goes.

I recently went jogging early in the morning, combining my prayers with exercise as I often do. I was deep in thought, staring vacantly at the pavement as I ran, when I looked up. Suddenly I was overwhelmed by the beauty of the sky, the sunlight dancing on exotic cloud formations, trees everywhere, squirrels, people, and the sound and sight of birds. I had been seeing only concrete and parked cars, while evidence of the majesty of God surrounded me! But is this not a picture of us all? We are surrounded everywhere by the miracle of creation. We live in the presence of the God of grace. And what do we do? Instead of being filled with wonder and praise we let other things shape our vision of life.

## A Community of Faith

When Jesus asked the rich young man to sell what he had and give to the poor, he did not invite him to become destitute and friendless, Richard Taylor has noted, but to join a community of faith and love.[7]

The importance of prayer and solitude excepted, our journey with God should never be taken alone or the culture of mammon is sure to overwhelm us. We are not lone rangers. We are made for life in community and we need to walk the way with others. We need their support and they need ours. That usually means family and friends, but it should always include an external community of faith where the gospel is truly celebrated and lives of service fostered. The temptation to make our spiritual journey a private quest may be characteristically American, a reflection of excessive individualism. And it may be rationalized by a prideful inability to find a church that meets our expectations. But the church is a fellowship of sinners whose lives are as flawed as our own. What binds us together is one Lord, one faith, one baptism.

A religious trend at the turn of the millennium in North America showed movement toward self-defined spirituality detached from "organized religion"—unorganized religion, by implication, being superior. This is "faith alone" with a new twist, the "bowling alone" syndrome applied to religious life, a cafeteria style of spiritual nourishment. But the private pursuit of transcendence or holiness (if that is what the individual wishes to pursue) does not stand up well under scrutiny for a number of reasons.

First, and at the heart of the issue, are truth claims. The main reason for anchoring our lives with others is not social enjoyment or encouragement (though neither is to be despised), but for nurture in the things of God—the truth of God. When truth is seen to be relative, one idea of truth is as good as another, because it is subjective and emerges from within each person. But if truth is established by God, and if truth is ultimately the revelation of God in Jesus, as the church confesses, then the place to pursue a life of faith is where that truth is believed and cultivated.

Second, God calls us to a community of faith. Jesus said "where two or three come together in my name, there am I with them" (Matt. 18:20). God in Christ is present every-where, but has not chosen to reveal that presence to us in the same way everywhere. Christ lives in each believer, but he promised to be present in a special way in the assembly of believers, and to make his presence known in the break-ing of bread and sharing of the cup (a sacramental pres-ence). The worship, the liturgy of the church, is a foretaste of the heavenly feast that links us with the saints and angels and all the company of heaven.

Third, the gathering of the faithful is part of the rhythm of life. Corporate worship is work, and work is worship, each requiring the other. Gathered, we are nourished for our work in the world, and living sacrificially in the world is our spiritual worship (Rom. 12:1–2). Both gathered in worship and scattered in the world, the church is in mis-sion, living and sharing the gospel. To believe in Christ is to be part of that mission and to support it in every way possible.

It is easy to reject the church for its flaws, which are great and many, and each of us has probably been tempted to do so at one time or another. Theologian Jaraslov Pelikan used to tell us in seminary that the church is like Noah's ark. The stench can be terrible, but it keeps us afloat. The problem with rejecting the church for its flaws is that *we* are no less flawed. Like other institutions, the church tends to be tol-erant of its shortcomings; but so are we regarding our own.

We readily ignore or excuse them. The flaws of others seem ever so much more offensive by comparison. But this view is self-righteous. The church is the communion of sinners, while simultaneously the communion of saints; and as forgiven sinners, we are both. We are called to be part of a fellowship of sinful saints, a more humble calling than that of standing aloof.

It has become common for people to "shop" for a church that meets their needs and to respond to problems in one congregation by moving to another. There is nothing wrong in looking for a church that meets the needs of your family. But every congregation has its problems, and we grow in commitment by assisting one another. We have some responsibility for helping our own congregation deal with its problems.

To be a religious loner is to separate oneself from the body of Christ and to miss the magnificent truth that in the Christian community we seek to come under God's reign. To choose absence from church is to take a stand that appears to reject rather than confess Christ. And often it is to misunderstand the purpose of worship, which is not to entertain or please ourselves, but among other things, to give collective praise to God. Neglect worship and our hearts are more open to clutter, more susceptible to mammon.

## Celebrating Grace

When Jesus startled his disciples by saying it is easier for a camel to go through a needle's eye than for a rich person to enter the kingdom, they asked, "Who then can be saved?" Jesus replied, "What is humanly impossible is possible with God" (Luke 18:26–27). That is a word of grace, because one thing we cannot do is bring mammon into total submission. Therefore only the mercy of God can save us.

A Christmas card I received has the following message:

172

> How wonderful it is to know that our hope
> is not based on what we can do for God
> but on what Christ has done for us.
> How deep is His peace . . . how great is His love!

The message is beautiful and true. It is the message of grace. But grace has a purpose. Grace must find expression in life, otherwise it is cheapened, its value despised, like an impoverished beggar who receives a fortune in bank notes only to light a match to it to warm his hands. Grace was celebrated, however, when Zacchaeus gave up most of his wealth in response to Jesus.

Oskar Schindler, a German industrialist, was honored in Israel as a "righteous Gentile" for having saved thousands of Jews from the Holocaust during World War II. He employed Jews in factories that made flawed and therefore useless armaments for the Nazis. But in the movie *Schindler's List,* when his factory workers were liberated, he broke into tears, saying, "I could have gotten more out. . . . I didn't do enough."[8] He was right. He was a courageous man, but he could have done more. Every one of us can say that.

When I look at my life, and when you look at yours, we find evidence that the culture of mammon has taken its toll. What do we see? So much indifference to the suffering of others and so many privileges for ourselves. So much more that we could have done. It is enough to make God weep. There is a mountain of evidence to sink any one of us when standing before the judgment of God. But that is not the last word. The last word is that in Christ God has taken the judgment for us on the cross. Consequently, we live by grace. God's Son has set us free to celebrate the gift of grace by seeking to return to God and to others all that we can.

Jesus said, "If you have faith as small as a mustard seed, you can say to this mountain, 'Move from here to there' and it will move" (Matt. 17:20–21). God uses even our tiny faith, when acted on, to accomplish great good.

173

We are like a four-year-old, drawing a picture and offering it to her daddy. "Beautiful!" the father announces. With the same delight, God also accepts the flawed offerings of our lives. "Beautiful!" says God, who sees not the flaws but the love, made perfect in Christ, that lies behind them.

FOURTEEN

# The Meek
# Inherit the Earth

Jesus was remarkably out of step with prevailing values. It was true then; it is true today. The rich and powerful are in deep trouble with God, he said. The poor, the lowly, and the despised are honored and welcome in the kingdom. The affluent are no less welcome, but they have to leave their baggage behind.

The call of Jesus and his invitation to the kingdom is good news for everyone, but it goes to everyone on the same terms. Both rich and poor, devout and derelict need to repent, to trust God with all their heart, and to let go of anything that imprisons them—money, pride, worry, hopelessness, whatever it may be. The rich are asked to humble themselves before God, the poor to believe they are exalted in Christ. All of us are asked to do both.

That is not exactly the wisdom of the world.

175

In our world, it is clearly those with money, power, and talent who get ahead. Yet Jesus said, "Blessed are the meek, for they will inherit the earth" (Matt. 5:5). The beatitudes reflect a fundamental paradox: mammon is ours, the earth is ours, life is ours—if we return them to God. This is nonsense to the world, which knows that "to the victor belong the spoils."

I heard a radio interview with an author of a book about insider-trading scandals on Wall Street. He said there are two sets of conflicting messages that Americans hear, starting in childhood. One says, "Do good, be honest, and obey the law." The other says, "Take what you can for yourself." In the world of male achievers, he observed, the second of the two messages predominates. For example, what do fraternity brothers talk about when they sit down for a beer? Does anyone ever say, "I had a chance to make a killing, but I decided to be honest instead"? No, they brag about how they have made a killing. The same applies when they move out into the world that includes Wall Street. They want to make it. There is even something exciting about leading a double life—outwardly a conservative, respectable businessman but inwardly working all the angles to get rich. People seldom ask, "How did you make the money?" They just say, "He made a bundle and is a great success."

A similar application could be made regarding sexual values and behavior, or the pursuit of fame, or power. I describe the culture of mammon a bit crassly. Perhaps most of us want to make it, to enjoy the symbols of success, but hope to do so honestly. When my oldest son, Nathan, was a teenager, he told me that he had decided to become a stockbroker, a millionaire by age thirty, and retire in the Bahamas. I told him I would be deeply hurt to see him fail so badly. (At age thirty, struggling to support a family, he thanked me for the conversation.)

The world tells us that the aggressive inherit the earth, and we are probably inclined to believe that it is so. A cartoon in the *The New Yorker* showed a portly man and his wife admiring scenic fields and trees through the picture window of their living room. The man says: "God's country? Well, I suppose it is. But I own it."[1] We laugh because the man is a caricature of ourselves.

It still jars me to see how casually we affluent Christians accept our own comparative luxury, while others have almost nothing. I am appalled that I take my own privileges largely for granted and consider so little the suffering of others. Surely the spirit of mammon lives not only within the secular carriers of our culture, but also within the church, within ourselves. We want our piece of the earth.

But, says Jesus, it is the meek who inherit the earth.

## Who Are the Meek?

*Webster's New World Dictionary* defines meek as (1) patient and mild; not inclined to anger or resentment; and (2) too submissive; easily imposed on; spineless; spiritless. The second definition probably gives the most common understanding—"meek" is not usually a compliment—but it is laughable to think that Jesus meant to applaud the spineless. The first definition is clearly related to what Jesus had in mind. But is that all he meant by meek?

Psalm 37, from which the beatitude is taken, urges trust in the Lord despite the apparent success of wicked men. Soon the wicked will be no more, the psalmist says. "But the meek will inherit the land and enjoy great peace" (v. 11 NIV). The psalmist also promises inheritance of the land to "those who hope in the Lord" (v. 9 NIV), are "righteous" (v. 29 NIV), and "wait for the Lord and keep his way" (v. 34 NIV).

Far from suggesting excessive submission to others, meekness means submission to God, which gives strength for obedience. Moses is called "more humble ["meek" in some translations] than anyone else on the face of the earth" (Num. 12:3 NIV). He was not being called a sissy. Nor did the astonishing compassion and dedication of Jesus to his mission suggest someone ready to wilt before a challenge. These virtues he received from God and offered totally to God. That he carried his obedience to the cross for our sake defined the meekness of Jesus as extraordinary courage.

We are now called to receive the mind of Christ and follow him. This is the way of meekness for us. The virtues he lived are ours to imitate.

In blessing the meek, Jesus is lifting up not the acquisitive and well-connected, but the poor, the powerless, and those more often oppressed than successful, who typically wind up on the underside of social respectability. Most of us, myself included, have a hard time accepting this eagerly, and a hard time receiving the gift of the kingdom as really good news, because we are among the privileged. It is hard to seize a disturbing truth when a comfortable life depends on toning it down. Perhaps that is why, as John Haughey has observed, "We read the Gospel as if we had no money, and we spend our money as if we know nothing of the Gospel."[2]

The socially and economically disenfranchised have less about which to feel self-sufficient and seem more eager to welcome the good news that God wants us to enter the kingdom. It is no coincidence, then, that the poorest fifth of the U.S. population consistently gives a higher proportion of income to charitable causes than do middle- and upper-income groupings. Most of us are poor in generosity rather than in spirit, for to recognize our spiritual poverty and the riches of God's grace leads to generosity. What would happen if we *really* became meek? What if we showed extravagant generosity with God's gifts to us? How much more empowered our lives and the mission of the church would be. And how much less suffering the world would have. Jesus said, "Where your treasure is, there your heart will be also" (Luke 12:34). By that standard, mammon appears to have a clear edge. We are not so meek after all.

The examples of Jesus and Moses teach us that to be meek is not to be shorn of ambition, but to have one's ambition transformed from self-serving purposes to that of serving God. Much has been made recently of an obscure prayer of a man named Jabez who asked the Lord to "bless me and enlarge my territory" (1 Chron. 4:10 NIV), a prayer that is being held up as a model for Christians.[3] If the intent is truly to ask God to enlarge opportunities for love and service, such a prayer is to be fervently offered, for that is ambition transformed. But if, set in our mammon-driven culture, the focus is on *me* and *my* territory, and the underlying intent is to use God to gain more for myself, it is an exercise in self-deception and in capitulation to urges that are anything but meek. "It is a scandal and a sin to ask God for more when we are not being faithful with what we have," writes Peter Larsen.[4] The model prayer for meekness and other virtues of the kingdom remains the Lord's Prayer.

"The earth is the LORD's, and everything in it" (Ps. 24:1 NIV). Those who acknowledge this by placing their hope in God and offering what they are and what they have to him and to his children in need—those are the meek. To them the promise is given—inherit the earth.

## Inherit the Kingdom

If Jesus tells the meek that the earth will belong to them, why did he say, as also recorded in the Sermon on the Mount, *not* to gather earthly treasures?

Do not store up for yourselves treasures on earth, where moth and rust destroy, and where thieves break in and steal. But store up for yourselves treasures in heaven, where moth and rust do not destroy, and where thieves do not break in and steal. For where your treasure is, there your heart will be also.

MATTHEW 6:19-21

179

These words bring us back to the paradox that we find life by giving it to Christ. To inherit the earth, we must let go of the earth. To obtain the earth, we must give earthly treasures away and place our heart elsewhere.

There are two sides to this paradox. The first is that letting go of the earth is to acknowledge that the earth belongs to the Lord. In that recognition comes the realization that the earth, all of it, is a gift for us to treasure, care for, and enjoy. The person who is preoccupied with mammon focuses on microscopic bits of the earth: a piece of property, a position, a bank account, a house, a closet full of clothes. Even the richest of the rich, or the most powerful of the powerful, garner a pathetically small fraction of the earth. They can become so engrossed in possessing what they call "mine" that they lose sight of the fact that they are stewards, not owners. They then mistake their identity, forgetting that they were made in the image of God and therefore also belong to God. (Caesar's image is on the coin, so Caesar gets his tax—but God gets what is stamped with God's image.)

Rich or poor, being captive to mammon means failing to see the earth as God's gift. A person may smile smugly and say, "The world is my oyster," but what he or she really means is, "Look at this tiny speck of earth that I have succeeded in making my own!" Such an appreciation of the earth turns a person toward self rather than toward God, robbing one of gratitude and joy.

The second side of the paradox is that the things of the earth will not last. Its treasures are subject to decay and to theft. Rich people, too, will decay—but this they forget in their preoccupation with mammon. Therefore, the only lasting treasures (whether money, time, ability, or influence) are those invested in heaven—that is to say, those given to help others, those put in service for the needy, those shared with the poor, those furthering the mission of the church, those protecting the earth for future generations. These, offered to God, have transcendent value. First John tells us not to love the world of sinful craving and pride: "The world and its desires pass away, but whoever does the will of God lives forever" (2:17). In a similar vein, the letter of James tells us:

> Believers in humble circumstances ought to take pride in their high position. But the rich should take pride in their humiliation—they will pass away like a wild flower.

JAMES 1:9–10

We inherit the earth by seeing it with the eyes of faith. Because we are part of God's new creation in Christ, we can perceive the world as it really is, and as it one day will be when, in the resurrection, the reign of God is fully revealed.

When the heart is given to God, mammon becomes a servant. We can then place it among other things to be enjoyed and used in a way that honors the God to whom everything belongs. And God, in turn, honors us not simply with the earth, but with the kingdom as our inheritance. A house, a bed, a family meal, friendships, work, prayer, pleasure, income, citizenship—these and all other things are changed, their value dramatically enhanced because they are accepted as treasures to enjoy and employ for the highest of purposes.

The God who richly loves us and has made this so evident in Christ opens his heart and wants to give us more than we can possibly fathom. We instinctively reach for something ridiculously small, but God says, "Inherit the earth." We may wish for passing advantages, but God says, "Inherit the kingdom." They are not different promises, but one and the same. Why should we ever wish for something so insignificant and transient as wealth or fame when God offers us the kingdom as an inheritance? And to celebrate the kingdom, why would we not gladly die to our privileges so that others may live?

181

The Roman conquerors, and all conquerors before and after them, fought, suffered, and risked death for the sake of treasure and a taste of fleeting glory. But in Christ, we have a glory from God that is lasting, and one that is incomparably superior. The brief reach of the Romans for glory prompted them to great sacrifice. They did it for a culture of death. We do it for life—for a crown that lasts forever.

# Postscript

## A FEW SUGGESTIONS

This is not a how-to book. The underlying need, it seems to me, is not for advice on things to do, but for people of faith to grasp that faith more fully and follow Christ more devoutly. How you do that will vary greatly according to individual circumstances. With this in mind, I offer a few possibilities, hoping they may prompt your own initiatives.

1. *Begin and continue with prayer.* Ask God for the courage to follow Jesus and for the wisdom to do it well.

2. *Decide on some steps, small ones at first, that allow your faith to become more active in love.* Do not try to become a St. Francis overnight. Begin with a few simple things, such as deciding on ways to be more kind to members of your family, setting aside a time for prayer, engaging with a family that needs help, and giving more to church and charity. But act, do not postpone. And whatever your steps are, take them as initial steps on a long journey.

3. *Deepen your devotional life.* Set a regular time and place for prayer, reflection, and Bible reading. Try to read other literature, including occasional books, that will help you understand and live your faith. The publisher of this book

and other publishers rooted in the Christian tradition can be of help.

4. *Discuss your intentions and progress with others.* Doing so will help you, but it will help them, as well. Your family and close friends are usually the best ones to start with. One reader of the initial draft of this book advises collaborating with your spouse first, if you are married, to avoid marital trouble. Another reader suggests inviting a handful of people to your home to discuss using finances and time more effectively.

5. *Do zero-based, faith-based budgeting.* If you were starting from scratch, how much of your income and possessions would you really need? Perhaps you need a smaller house. Or perhaps you can use your house to welcome additional guests, such as foreign students, neighbors, and people who are not on anyone else's guest list; you might use these occasions to share your love and—maybe in the context of an after-dinner devotion—tell your guests why you want to become a more loving person. One small example, but you get the idea.

6. *Do that zero-based, faith-based budgeting also with the use of your time, your talent, and the influence that you have.* These are all huge gifts and God has ideas about how you can use them. One of God's gifts is to make you struggle to figure out what those ideas are, for in the process of doing so you will grow in faith and service.

7. *Give special thought to your role in the church and its mission.* How can you be engaged in mission locally? How can you support the church's mission elsewhere and internationally with your gifts and prayers?

8. *Give special consideration to the most vulnerable.* This includes the hungry, the homeless, the friendless, prisoners (including ex-offenders and families of prisoners), the unborn, and those born but left to grow up with few opportunities and little guidance.

184

9. *Give wisely.* At Christmas, we tend to give things not needed to people not in need. Exercise restraint. Keep the focus on Christ. Give at least as much to the poor as to the prosperous. Get personally involved with someone or some family in need.

10. *Begin to see the world through the eyes of God.* Practice relating to others through the heart and mind of Christ.

11. *Turn off the TV.*

12. *Spend more time with family.*

13. *Help your children from the youngest age on up learn the joy of giving.* And the joy of numbers nine and ten on this list.

14. *Take care of God's creation.* Practice and encourage conservation of energy and resources. Drive less, turn out lights, lower the thermostat, and ask elected officials to adopt energy-saving policies. Recycle paper, plastic, glass, and aluminum cans. Add as little pollution as possible. Get your family and community involved, as well. Support anti-pollution measures with state and national legislators.

15. *Have a heart for the world.* Keep up on events and pray about them. Contribute generously for overseas relief and development. Use your power as a citizen to let elected officials, especially your national legislators, know that you would like your country to take the lead in helping to end hunger and reduce poverty in the world. An advocacy group such as Bread for the World can help you do this. Remember that public affairs as well as private life come under the lordship of Christ and have an enormous impact on the well-being of others.

16. *Make out your will so that what you leave behind continues to fulfill the mission of Christ.*

17. *Do what you do with joy and thanksgiving as a celebration of God's grace.* Returning to God and sharing with others the treasure of life becomes a delight.

18. *Consider Jesus your most trusted advisor.* As you struggle to offer your life more completely and effectively to God, ask, "What would Jesus want me to do?" You seldom get a

direct or immediate answer, of course, but prayerful reading of the Bible sure helps.

19. *Avoid at all costs the temptation to become self-righteous.* Nothing ruins an otherwise good thing faster than pride. Trust me, you will always have plenty of reason for humility.

As I said, these are just a few ideas to stimulate your own. The main obstacle, of course, is not a shortage of ideas, but shortage of will. So as you work this out, remember that "it is God who works in you to will and to act according to his good purpose" (Phil. 2:13). God will use your simple acts of obedience to strengthen your will to continue on.

# Notes

### Chapter 1: That Seductive Urge

1. *Mammon* is Aramaic, the language spoken by Jesus, and was carried over into the Greek and English languages.

### Chapter 2: Fat Wallets, Empty Lives

1. Gerard Thomas Straub, *The Sun and Moon over Assisi: A Personal Encounter with Francis and Clare* (Cincinnati: St. Anthony Messenger Press, 2000), 115.

2. John F. Cavanaugh, *Following Christ in a Consumer Society*, revised edition (Maryknoll, N.Y.: Orbis, 1991), 59.

3. John and Sylvia Ronsvalle, *The Poor Have Faces* (Grand Rapids: Baker, 1992), 43.

4. Cited by Will Willimon, "Jesus Visits the Hamptons," *Sojourners*, March/April 2002, 36–38.

5. Don McClanen and Dale Stitt, *Ministry of Money*, October 1989, 3.

6. Richard J. Foster, *Celebration of Discipline* (New York: Harper & Row, 1978), 73.

### Chapter 3: Hope and Purpose

1. Richard J. Foster, *Streams of Living Water* (San Francisco: HarperSanFrancisco, 1998), 51.

2. Carol Morello, "From Front Lines to Back Roads," *Washington Post*, 11 March 2002, A-1.

3. John Piper, *Desiring God* (Sisters, Ore.: Multnomah, 1986), 219.

4. Philip Sherrard, "Sacred Cosmology and the Ecological Crisis," in *Simpler Living, Compassionate Life*, ed. Michael Schut (Denver: The Morehouse Group, 1999), 201.

5. Rhodes Thompson, *Stewards Shaped by Grace* (St. Louis: Chalice, 1990), vii.

6. Ibid., 117.

7. Quoted by Jim Hoagland, "Help Us," *Washington Post*, 22 August 1999, B-7.

## Chapter 4: Rushing to Nowhere

1. Cited by Bruce C. Birch and Larry L. Rasmussen, *The Predicament of the Prosperous* (Philadelphia: Westminster, 1978), 41.
2. Alexis de Tocqueville, *Democracy in America*, ed. J. P. Mayer and Max Lerner, trans. George Lawrence (New York: Harper & Row, 1966), 508, 510.
3. Louis Uchitelle, "Working Families Strain to Live Middle-Class Life," *New York Times*, 10 September 2000, A-1.
4. Bob Herbert, "Focus on Women," *New York Times*, 28 September 2000, A-op.ed.
5. "Currents," *The Lutheran*, September 2000, 9.
6. Cited by John Haughey, *The Holy Use of Money* (New York: Crossroads, 1989), 137.
7. Larry Burkett, "Business Bondage," *Money Matters*, September 2001, 9.
8. Four hours and thirty-two minutes per day was the average adult daily viewing time for the 2000–2001 season, according to Nielsen Media Research. Reported on 10 April 2002, by Jo LaVerde of Nielsen Media Research, in an e-mail to the author.
9. David G. Myers, *The Pursuit of Happiness* (New York: William Morrow, 1992), 136–37.
10. Søren Kierkegaard, *Works of Love*, translated by Howard and Edna Hong, cited by Martin E. Marty in *Context*, 1 November 2000, 8.
11. Søren Kierkegaard, *Purity of Heart Is to Will One Thing*, translated by Douglas V. Steere (New York: Harper & Brothers, 1956).
12. Interview of James C. Dobson, "The Family in Crisis," *Focus on the Family*, August 2001, 4.

13. Rodney Clapp, "The Theology of Consumption & the Consumption of Theology," in *The Consuming Passion: Christianity & the Consumer Culture*, ed. Rodney Clapp (Downers Grove: InterVarsity, 1998), 199–200.
14. Fernando Cardenal, quoted in *Ministry of Money*, December 2000, 9.
15. Walter Brueggemann, "The Liturgy of Abundance, the Myth of Scarcity," *The Christian Century*, 24–31 March 1999, 342ff.
16. A 37.5 hour week has become increasingly common for many in the U.S., while others are expected to work much beyond that. In biblical times and in developing countries today twelve- to fourteen-hour work days are common, often for young children as well. I have been told that South Carolina was the first state (then a colony) to legislate work limitations; it limited work to sixteen hours a day.
17. Marva J. Dawn, *Keeping the Sabbath Wholly* (Grand Rapids: Eerdmans, 1989), 146.
18. Based on 1998 data as reported to the author on 8 April 2002, by Heather Jue of Mediascope, a nonprofit media research organization based in Studio City, California.

## Chapter 5: The Poverty of Riches

1. See Matthew 6:24–34 and Luke 12:22–31.
2. James Fallows, "The Invisible Poor," *The New York Times Magazine*, 19 March 2000, 68.
3. Dom Helder Camara, *Revolution through Peace* (New York: Harper & Row, 1971), cited by Gladys M. Hunt, "Evangelism and Simpler Life Style," in *Living More Simply*, ed. Ronald J. Sider (Downers Grove: InterVarsity, 1980), 171.

4. From the hymn, "God of Grace and God of Glory," by Harry Emerson Fosdick, *Lutheran Book of Worship* (Minneapolis: Augsburg, 1978), hymn 415.

5. C. S. Lewis, *The Weight of Glory and Other Addresses* (Grand Rapids: Eerdmans, 1965), 1–2.

6. Cited by Richard J. Foster, *Freedom of Simplicity* (San Francisco: Harper & Row, 1981), 105.

7. Reinhold Niebuhr, *An Interpretation of Christian Ethics* (New York: Meridian, 1956), 47.

8. Cited by Edward W. Bauman, *Where Your Treasure Is* (Arlington, Va.: Bauman Bible Telecasts, 1980), 103–4.

9. Cited in *Ministry of Money*, August 1990, 4. Menninger also said that generous people are seldom mentally ill.

10. Thomas Cahill, *Desire of the Everlasting Hills: The World Before and After Jesus* (New York: Doubleday, 1999), 193.

11. Dietrich Bonhoeffer, *The Cost of Discipleship* (New York: Macmillan, 1963), 197.

12. Walter Brueggemann, *The Prophetic Imagination*, 2d ed. (Minneapolis: Fortress, 2001), 1.

13. John C. Haughey, *The Holy Use of Money: Personal Finances in Light of Christian Faith*, revised (New York: Crossroads, 1989), 17.

14. *Repentance:* a change of heart and mind in which we turn to God and away from all that separates us from God and neighbor. *Faith:* full trust in God for life and for salvation.

15. Don McClanen, "Stewardship Challenges for Ministering to Affluent Persons," undated pamphlet by Ministry of Money, Gaithersburg, Md.

16. Reverend Pamela Stephenson, "Overcome by Love." This poem appeared in a slightly altered form in *Ministry of Money* (February 1989). Used by permission of the author.

17. Ron Sider, ed., *Living More Simply* (Downers Grove: InterVarsity, 1980), 12–13.

**Chapter 6: The Sorrow of Pleasure**

1. Lawrence C. Brennan, "Roman Catholics Speaking the Gospel into Postmodern Ears," *Concordia Journal*, April 2001, 116.

2. Quoted by J. D. McClatchy, "Like a Moth to the Flame," *The New York Times Book Review*, 16 September 2001, 12.

3. Daniel Goleman, *Emotional Intelligence*, reported by David Gergen, "The 50 Percent Catastrophe," *U.S. News & World Report*, 2 October 1995, 58.

4. Philip Yancey, "The 'Ample' Man Who Saved My Faith," *Christianity Today*, 3 September 2001, 70. Excerpted and adapted from his book, *Soul Survivor* (New York: Doubleday, 2001).

5. C. S. Lewis, *God in the Dock* (Grand Rapids: Eerdmans, 1970), 280.

6. Douglas L. Rutt, "The Joy and Peace of Knowing Jesus," *Touched by His Word* series (St. Louis: Concordia, 2001), 1–2.

**Chapter 7: The Weakness of Power**

1. Quoted in Thomas Cahill, *Pope John XXIII* (New York: Viking Penguin, 2002), ix.

2. I substitute "everything" for "good and evil" as the translation, because the expression, "knowing good and evil," in other places in the

Old Testament means knowing everything from A to Z (omniscience).

3. Quoted by Trevor Roper in the introduction to Lord Acton, *Lectures on Modern History* (London: Collins, 1960), 13.

4. Henri Nouwen, *In the Name of Jesus: Reflections on Christian Leadership* (New York: Crossroads, 1989), 59.

5. Reinhold Niebuhr, *The Irony of American History* (New York: Charles Scribner's Sons, 1952), 37.

6. Jonathan Kozol, "Spare Us the Cheap Grace," *Time*, 11 December 1995, 96.

7. William Wilberforce, *Real Christianity*, quoted in "Reflections," *Christianity Today*, 26 April 1999, 105.

### Chapter 8: Faces of Affluence

1. For a more extensive introduction to this topic, see David Beckmann and Arthur Simon, *Grace at the Table: Ending Hunger in God's World* (New York: Paulist Press; Downers Grove: InterVarsity, 1999).

2. All figures are in year 2000 U.S. dollars, so the 1900 numbers are adjusted for inflation. The figures are based on a 17 May 2002 e-mail to the author from Xiao Ye, a research analyst at the World Bank. The 2000 figure is firm. The 1900 figure is a very rough guess, based on the Bank's 1960 figure of $9 trillion in world economic output and Xiao Ye's comment, "If the historical trend means anything, a simple-minded average gives up about 1.5 trillion current dollar estimate in 1900."

3. Cited by Tom Sine, *The Mustard Seed Conspiracy* (Waco: Word, 1981), 82.

4. Cited by Ched Myers, *The Biblical Vision of Sabbath Economics* (Washington D.C.: Church of the Saviour, 2001), 17.

5. David S. Landes, *The Wealth and Poverty of Nations* (New York: W. W. Norton, 1998), xx.

6. Ibid.

7. *A Future with Hope: Hunger 2002*, twelfth annual report on the state of world hunger (Washington, D.C.: Bread for the World Institute, 2001), 9.

8. Barbara Ehrenreich, *Nickled and Dimed: On (Not) Getting By in America* (New York: Holt, 2001).

### Chapter 9: How Much Is Enough?

1. Rachel Alexander, "For Venus, a Grand Finale," *Washington Post*, 10 September 2000, D-1.

2. See, for example, David Brooks, *Bobos in Paradise: The New Upper Class and How They Got There* (New York: Simon & Schuster, 2000), and Alan Wolfe, *Moral Freedom: The Search for Virtue in A World of Choice* (New York: Norton, 2000).

3. David Steindl-Rast and Sharon Lebell, *Music of Silence*, quoted by Gerard Thomas Straub, *The Sun & Moon over Assisi: A Personal Encounter with Frances and Clare* (Cincinnati: St. Anthony Messenger Press, 2000), 169.

4. Tom Sine, *Why Settle for More and Miss the Best?* (Waco: Word, 1987).

5. David G. Myers, *The Pursuit of Happiness* (New York: William Morrow, 1992), 51ff.

6. David G. Myers, *The Pursuit of Happiness* (New York: William Morrow, 1992), 56.

7. Gerard Thomas Straub, *The Sun & Moon over Assisi: A Personal Encounter with Frances and Clare* (Cincinnati: St. Anthony Messenger Press, 2000), 522.

8. Cited by John Piper, *Desiring God* (Sisters, Ore.: Multnomah, 1986), 211.

9. See also Deuteronomy 28, which expands on this point and warns that curses will also follow disobedience. This supported the viewpoint that misfortune was a sign of judgment against some sin, and wealth a mark of virtue.

10. "The poor you will always have with you," (Mark 14:7) is sometimes cited as a statement of Jesus to indicate the opposite, but that understanding would contradict all other clear words of Jesus on this. The occasion is a woman pouring a jar of extremely costly perfume on his head shortly before his death, prompting his disciples to protest that the money could instead have been given to the poor. Jesus defended her for the very special circumstances and her extravagant love. The reaction of his disciples showed that he had taught them well.

11. Marva Dawn, "This birth makes us odd," *The Lutheran*, December 2001, 6.

12. Dietrich Bonhoeffer, *The Cost of Discipleship* (New York: Macmillan, 1963 edition), 90.

13. Ronald J. Sider, *Rich Christians in an Age of Hunger*, rev. ed. (Dallas: Word, 1997).

14. Daniel Kadlec, "Quiet Giver," *Time*, 17 September 2001, 62–63.

## Chapter 10: Living Simply So That Others May Simply Live

1. Cited by David Neff, "Keeping Up with the Huxtables," *Books & Culture*, September/October 1998, 5. Taken from Juliet Schor, *The Overspent American* (New York: Basic Books, 1998).

2. Dietrich Bonhoeffer, *Ethics* (London: SCM Press, 1955), 95.

3. From the ELCA World Hunger Appeal.

4. Peter Singer, "The Singer Solution To World Poverty," *The New York Times Magazine*, 5 September 1999, 60–63. Singer's views on some matters, such as euthanasia and infanticide, are deplorable. But that someone such as Singer, with no hope in God, shows far more generosity to the poor than do most Christians is to our great shame.

5. These examples come from appeals received in the mail by the author from the Heifer Project International, Lutheran World Relief, and World Vision.

6. Marva J. Dawn, *Keeping the Sabbath Wholly* (Grand Rapids: Eerdmans, 1989), 184.

7. Rodger Charles, *Christian Social Witness and Teaching*, vol. 1 (Herefordshire, U.K.: Gracewing, 1998), 90.

8. Pope Paul VI, *On the Development of the Peoples* (Washington, D.C.: U.S. Catholic Conference, 1967), 10.

9. John E. Tropman, "Catholic & Protestant Ethics," in *The Consuming Passion*, ed. Rodney Clapp (Downers Grove: InterVarsity, 1998), 76.

10. Data obtained by the author by phone on 17 April 2002 from the Natural Resources Defense Council, a New York–based environmental research and advocacy organization.

## Chapter 11: Love and Justice

1. Jimmy Allen, "The Tears of God," *Christian Ethics Today*, February 2002, 6–7.

2. Janet Poppendieck, *Sweet Charity? Emergency Food and the End of*

*Entitlement* (New York: Viking, 1998), 221–22.

3. Peter J. Gomez, "A Pilgrim's Progress," *The New York Times Magazine*, 18 April 1999, 103.

4. Cited by Martin E. Marty in the Hastings Lecture at the National Cathedral in Washington, D.C., 17 November 2000.

5. Gordon Brown, "Marshall Plan for the Next 50 Years," *Washington Post*, 17 December 2001, A-23.

6. Jeffrey D. Sachs, "One-Tenth of 1 Percent to Make the World Safer," *The Washington Post*, 21 November 2001, A-op.ed.

7. Paul Simon, "Human Element Can Add Reality to Public Policy," *Chicago Sun-Times*, 22 August 2000, 27.

**Chapter 12: Saying "Yes" to Life**

1. Dietrich Bonhoeffer, *The Cost of Discipleship* (New York: MacMillan, 1963), 94.

2. Gerard Thomas Straub, from an essay to be published in his photo-essay book, *When Did I See You Hungry?* (Cincinnati: St. Anthony Messenger Press, 2003).

3. David Beckmann, memo to the author, 2 September 2000.

**Chapter 13: Filling the Heart with Something Better than Cash**

1. See James W. Skillen, *A Covenant to Keep: Meditations on the Biblical Theme of Justice* (Grand Rapids: CRC Publications, 2000), 47.

2. Don Latin, "The Publisher Meets the Preacher," *The Lutheran*, 5 November 1986, 9.

3. Richard J. Foster, *Celebration of Discipline* (New York: Harper & Row, 1978), 35.

4. Gary Arndt, "Contemplative Social Action," *Bread for the World in Louisiana* (June 2001), 1. Reprinted from *Just Peace Journal*, May/June 2001.

5. Jean Vanier, *Eruption to Hope* (New York: Paulist Press, 1971), 63.

6. Patrick Jordan, 19 August 2000.

7. Richard K. Taylor, *Economics and the Gospel*, cited by Ronald J. Sider, *Rich Christians in an Age of Hunger*, revised (Dallas: Word, 1990), 73.

8. *Schindler's List*, dir. Steven Spielberg, Universal Studios, 1993.

**Chapter 14: The Meek Inherit the Earth**

1. Cited by Frank E. Gaebelein, "Old Testament Foundations for Living More Simply," in *Living More Simply*, ed. Ronald J. Sider, (Downers Grove: InterVarsity Press, 1980), 27.

2. John Haughey, *Virtue and Affluence: The Challenge of Wealth* (Kansas City: Sheed & Ward, 1997), cited by Ched Myers, *The Biblical Vision of Sabbath Economics* (Washington D.C.: Church of the Saviour, 2001), 5.

3. Bruce Wilkinson, *The Prayer of Jabez* (Sisters, Ore.: Multnomah, 2000).

4. Peter Larsen, "Who Needs Jesus When You've Got Jabez?" *Prism*, Sept/Oct 2001, 28.